GOD'S WORD EXPRESSED IN HUMAN WORDS

The Bible's Literary Forms

God's Word Expressed in Human Words

The Bible's Literary Forms

Michael D. McGehee

A Liturgical Press Book

 THE LITURGICAL PRESS
Collegeville, Minnesota

To my friends and colleagues:
Sr. Angelo Haspert, O.S.B., Sr. Shaun O'Meara, O.S.B.,
Prof. John Merkle, Sr. Mary Reuter, O.S.B.,
and Sr. Mary Anthony Wagner, O.S.B.,
with thanks for their encouragement and advice.

Cover design by Fred Petters.

1	2	3	4	5	6	7	8	9

Library of Congress Cataloging-in-Publication Data

McGehee, Michael David.
   God's word expressed in human words / Michael McGehee.
      p.   cm.
   ISBN 0-8146-2009-4
   1. Bible—Criticism, interpretation, etc. 2. Bible—Criticism,
Form.   I. Title.
BS511.2.M254 1991
220.6'6—dc20   90-27368
                                             CIP

Contents

Introduction:
If Jesus Told a Joke,
Would You Laugh?

Imagine a friend picking up a telephone book, showing it to you, and saying, "I just finished reading this great novel. Let me read some parts of it to you."

Imagine him opening to the middle of the book and starting to read the names, addresses, and phone numbers that appear under the letter *P*. If he were a talented reader who could modulate his voice, he might be able to read the names and numbers with a great deal of feeling, sometimes reading a name with disgust, sometimes with awe. Yet, even if he could read the names and express a different emotion for each name just by changing the tone of his voice, you would know that he was doing something odd. In fact, you would probably wonder if he was joking with you by this strange way of reading the phone book.

Figuring out how to describe what is odd about this way of reading the phone book depends on recognizing that somehow or other, your friend has made a mistake about the kind of thing he is reading. After all, even though the telephone book is like a novel in a number of ways, a telephone book is not a novel.

The telephone book and a novel both have people's names. But the phone book has more characters than even that classic but convoluted Russian novel *War and Peace*. There are all kinds of people in the phone book. There are heroes and villains, handsome men and beautiful women, blue-collar workers and executives, and on and on. Each one of them has a story. But the phone book does not tell us their stories. It does give us some information about each person. We can learn an address and a telephone number. But that sort of information is useful rather than interesting, and no one stays up late at night just to read columns of names and numbers. Any book critic who reviewed the phone book as if it were a novel would say that the plot was weak and that the characters were never really developed.

Nevertheless, even though phone books and novels both tell us things about the people whose names appear in their pages, the simple fact is that a phone book is not a novel. It is a list. Literate people familiar with telephones would not make the sort of mistake just described. Even without studying phone books in any high school or college classroom, literate people know that the phone book belongs to a different category of literature than a novel does. The word that means a category of literature is "genre" (pronounced *zhahn'ra*). The phone book belongs to a different genre than *War and Peace*.

Mistakes in genre do not happen very often in normal reading or conversation. Most of us can almost instantly recognize whether we are reading a sermon, a play, or a love letter. In fact, when we think of other possible mistakes in genre, they all seem farfetched. For example, we would think it odd if someone criticized *The Hobbit* because it did not describe the treatment hobbits needed for hypertension and went on to say that any decent medical book about hobbits should deal with that disease. In the same manner, we would wonder about the sanity of anyone who said that $x = 2y + 3z + 17$ had an unusual rhythm pattern for a limerick. Novels are not medical encyclopedias and equations are not limericks.

Yet there are times when confusion about genres can occur. That is how many jokes work. You might think you are hearing a true story and then realize that you have been listening to a joke. Still, this sort of genre misunderstanding does not happen regularly. At most we only need to hear a few words before we can recognize the difference between a joke, a fairy tale, a marriage proposal, or a request to turn down the television.

Literate people do not normally have problems with genre in the contemporary use of their native language. However, mistakes in genre often occur when we are exposed to a different language or to literature written in the past. Learning another language involves learning about different genres that might be common in that language. But reading ancient or medieval literature also requires that a person know something about the styles and types of writing that were in use during previous times. What makes understanding genres so important for Christians today is that the Bible combines both of these factors. The Bible was not written in English but in Hebrew and Greek, and, even worse, the most recent parts of it were written over 1,850 years ago.

Mistakes about genre occur so often when people study the Bible that most of us do not even notice them. For example, it does not take a lot of Sundays going to church or watching religious broadcasts on television to hear a statement like "The Bible teaches . . ."

First, before we go any further, let me make it clear that as a Christian I am very interested in what the Bible teaches. But how can one be sure that the Bible is really *teaching* something? How do I know whether, instead of teaching something, the Bible is stating it, or affirming it, or quoting it, or using it as part of a story to make some other point?

For example, the Bible does not *teach* that Christians are to obey Jesus when he says, "Go into the village opposite you, and as you enter it you will find a colt tethered on which no one has ever sat. Untie it and bring it here." (The quotation is from Luke 19:30, and, as all other biblical quotations, it is from the New American Bible.) Luke reports that Jesus gave this order to his disciples, but the order itself is part of the overall story about Jesus' entry into Jerusalem. If a person today were to take this report of Jesus' remark to his disciples as a *teaching* about how Christians were to behave, we would probably need a new ritual in our worship services: donkey untying.

This kind of absurdity in misinterpreting Jesus leads to the question that is the title of this introduction. If Jesus told a joke, would you laugh? I realize that this is an odd question and that some Christians might be uncomfortable with the idea that Jesus told jokes. But, assuming that he might have told one, would you laugh? It would depend on whether the joke was funny, of course. Given the fact, however, that Jesus was an experienced and successful public speaker, I think we can assume that any jokes he might have told would have been funny.

Getting back to the question asked in this chapter's title now forces us to face the problem of genre. How would a person know that she or he was hearing a joke?

In a face-to-face meeting it is not that hard. One can sometimes tell by the tone of a person's voice or by a smile that the other person is going to say something funny. And there are also verbal patterns to jokes that let us recognize that we are about to hear one. Every time I hear someone begin a story along the lines of "There were these two Irishmen, Pat and Mike, who . . . ," I expect a joke.

Sometimes a joke does not become clear until the punchline. That is when you finally realize that there was a pun hidden in the words that described the situation or that the incident being reported has turned into something incredible. In any case, though, you realize you are hearing a joke because of certain external or internal clues to the genre.

The importance of recognizing that there are different genres, which must be discovered by external and internal clues, is obvious when one considers how difficult it might be to read a long and complex book like the Bible. In any book of over a thousand pages, there may be all sorts of genres. And, unless we appreciate the genre of what we are reading, we may make the same mistake as the hypothetical person who read the phone book as if it were a novel.

Even quickly reading one of the four Gospels shows that there were a variety of things that Jesus did when he spoke. He did not spend all his time teaching, for example. He told parables, delivered sermons, engaged in dialogues, said blessings, gave orders, asked rhetorical questions, and rebuked people for wrong behavior. To figure out what Jesus meant in any given situation requires knowing something about what he intended to be doing with his words at that time. And, in the same manner, to discover what Paul (or Jeremiah or the psalmist) meant in a Scripture passage requires knowing the genre of that passage.

For example, taking a comment from one of Jesus' parables as if it were, in its most literal sense, a teaching about Christian behavior would surely mean misunderstanding what Jesus intended. When Jesus finished the parable of the Good Samaritan, recorded in Luke 10:25-37, he said, "Go and do likewise." He did not mean that Christians were to travel up and down the road from Jerusalem to Jericho looking for injured people so that they could drop them off in motels. Instead he meant that they were to help out those they meet who are in need.

In the rest of this book I am going to discuss a number of different genres that can be found in the Bible. After a brief explanation of each genre and some examples of it, I will comment on how Christians today might make sense of the other parables, hymns, law codes, genealogies, and so on, that make up the Scriptures. Occasionally I will mention how Christians have previously disagreed, or currently disagree, about the correct genre and proper interpretation of a passage.

Whatever else this book is, it is not Scripture, and I expect that a few readers will probably disagree with some of the interpretations presented here. But disagreements about how to interpret Scripture are nothing new and, in fact, appear to have been common, according to the New Testament itself, among the first Christians. My purpose in illustrating the variety of literature in the Bible and showing why it is important to understand that variety should not be taken as an attempt to weaken any believer's faith. My purpose instead is to discover, as much as we can, the original message the biblical authors attempted to communicate.

CHAPTER 1

Why Christians Argue So Much About the Bible

We all love to be right, to think that we have got the answers. It is probably as much a part of our human nature as is the desire for food or sleep. I do not see that there is any point in judging this very human trait to be either sinful or dangerous. For the desire to learn about things, to understand what we see, and to be correct in our thinking leads us to study both the world and ourselves. The truths discovered and expressed by geniuses as diverse as Emily Dickinson and Albert Einstein have their roots in our natural longing to understand.

The problem, however, comes when our desire to be right interferes with our actual ability to understand something that is complex. We prematurely claim understanding. When we should be continuing the process of learning and study, we close our minds to further inquiry. Then, to make things worse, we go from the belief that we are right to the conclusion that other people are wrong. And, if the truth that we think we have has something to do with religion, we not only think that other people are wrong but also that they are sinful and have closed their minds to God's truth.

This is not the place to go further into the psychological and sociological factors that influence our tendency to make premature conclusions. This is a book about how to read the Bible, and I want to keep the focus on how we can better our understanding of the Scriptures. Therefore, even though there are other factors involved in why Christians argue so much about the Bible, there are two primary mistakes Christians make in the actual process of reading the texts that lead to disagreements. These mistakes in reading then lead to all sorts of strange errors in interpreting the Bible.

The most common mistake made by people who read the Bible is "taking things out of context." By this I mean selecting a part of the Bible—what is selected can sometimes be as small as a single word but usually is a verse—and then getting a message out of this selection without any consideration of what went before it or what comes after it.

To see how absurd this approach is, we only need to consider what Jesus said in Luke 14:26: "If anyone comes to me without hating his father and mother, wife and children, brothers and sisters, and even his own life, he cannot be my disciple." Not for a minute do I believe that Jesus is teaching that Christians are supposed to hate their parents. Instead his statement in verse 26 must be seen in the broader context of the verses surround it. Likewise, in 1 Corinthians 15:33, where Paul says to eat, drink, and make merry because tomorrow we are to die, he is not explaining how Christians are to behave. Rather, he is quoting a slogan made by certain ancient philosophers in his development of a logical argument about the resurrection of Christ. Paul rejects the Epicurean view, and anyone who reads the whole of chapter 15 can easily see that he does.

These two examples are extreme, and I have yet to hear Christians seriously propose taking those two verses in the way just described. Yet Christians regularly select words, phrases, and verses they like and then ignore the surrounding material as they focus on the idea that happened to come to them while they were reading some particular word, phrase, or verse. The resulting theological interpretations can be as strange as taking Jesus' remark about hating your parents literally. The only way to avoid this error is to look at the context of the passage. But that is not as easy as it sounds.

Although taking individual words and phrases out of context seems without any logical explanation, the problem of taking verses out of context has, at one level, a rational basis. The Bible is usually presented in such a way that it is easy for us to misunderstand what we are reading. Most of our Bibles are printed with numbered chapters and verses running through every paragraph on every page. The mistake we make is looking upon these numbered verses as individual units of theological information. Each verse is assumed to have a significant meaning. After all, why would it have been given a unique number unless it had some special meaning that the reader was supposed to discover? Yet even though some verses do have that kind of freestanding and unique meaning, most verses can only be understood in their context.

The verse numbers that we have were not put in the Bible by the writers. They were placed in the text by the first printers and copyists, who needed a quick way of finding their way through hundreds of pages. The chapter and verse numbers in use today were not standardized until about 1560. Even though they help us move quickly from one passage to another, I think it is fair to say that the verse numbers, which were put into the text to help find and correct errors, actually caused more problems than they solved. The verse numbers helped printers find errors in spelling and word order, but they led to a very different sort of error by giving an almost mathematical foundation for simpleminded and legalistic interpretations of isolated verses.

Instead of reflecting on isolated verses, a reader who wants to understand an author's message should look at each verse in its context. There is a word to describe a unit of biblical material that is not taken out of context. That word is "pericope" (pronounced *per-ICK-oh-pee*). The word itself comes from two Greek words that mean "to cut around." A pericope is a unit of biblical material that can be marked off (cut around), so that when it is read there is a beginning, an end, and some sort of overall meaning. There are times when a single verse counts as a pericope, as in Proverbs, but usually a pericope is a larger collection of verses. For example, the verse about hating your father and mother fits into the pericope of Luke 14:25-33, in which Jesus explains the importance of the Christian life. The overall point seems to be that in comparison with our devotion to the gospel, all other affections are insignificant.

There are a few passages in the Bible where even the scholars differ on the beginning or end of a pericope. For example, should the pericope which begins in John 3:1 end at verse 10, verse 15, or verse 21? Such disagreements about the limits of pericopes are rare. Nevertheless, in the passages over which there are disagreements about a pericope's length, there can be wide differences of opinion about what is being said.

Recognizing that the context of a verse is crucial to interpreting anything in the Bible allows Christians a way to start a discussion on matters about which they disagree. If you have ever had someone quote Paul's phrase in Galatians 5:10, "I am confident of you in the Lord that you will not take a different view," out of context and use it in support of whatever is being discussed, you will realize the value of seeing that Paul's remark was part of an emotional appeal within the context of his argument for the validity of the gospel. Paul's statement cannot be used legitimately as a sort of religious land-claim, with whoever quotes it first concluding that they have staked out the boundaries of the truth.

As long as we Christians continue to disagree with one another by quoting isolated Bible verses at one another, we are never going to be able to engage in dialogue. This kind of behavior is often called a "verse war." It makes about as much sense as the children's card game of "War." There is no logic, skill, or intelligence involved in the play. What matters most is the cards you were dealt. The winner in the card game of "War" is usually whoever can sit there the longest, flipping up card after card, and the winner in a "verse war" is usually whoever can fire off the most verses.

But when we go beyond single verses and start to explore the message of a given pericope and say why we think that such-and-such interpretation is the best one, we will be able to talk. That does not mean that talk will lead to agreement. But it does suggest that we will be able to begin to understand where others are coming from.

The second most common mistake in reading the Bible is "taking the Bible literally." Everyone has heard this expression. But just what does it mean? I have never met or read or heard of anyone who took the Bible literally. Instead all Christians I have ever met, including the fundamentalists who *say* that they take the Bible literally, take parts of it literally and other parts of it figuratively. For example, few Protestant fundamentalists take Jesus literally when he says, "Whoever eats my flesh and drinks my blood has eternal life, and I will raise him on the last day" (John 6:54). The usual explanation among Protestants, including the Protestant fundamentalists, is that Jesus meant this comment about eating flesh and drinking blood in a figurative sense. There are Roman Catholics who do take this verse literally, but, at the same time, they usually interpret the New Testament references to Jesus' "brothers" as actually referring to his stepbrothers.

What makes talking with fundamentalists so difficult is that their claims to take the Bible literally are often operating at a less-than-conscious level, along with an effort to be (or a desire to seem) holier than other people. Since no one takes the Bible literally from cover to cover, groups of Christians differ instead on what they understand to be the figurative statements and the literal statements. When asked how they know which is which, the usual answer is "It's obvious."

Of course, another possible but equally unpersuasive answer is that the Holy Spirit has revealed it to them personally. People who use this second approach are saying, in effect, that they are given a special gift from God that you do not have and that you must just accept their word for it. You should not ask to have God reveal the truth to you, because that means doubting God.

Talking with other Christians who believe that they are hooked up to God's fax machine or who have different opinions about what is "obvious" can be very difficult. Since there is usually some sort of negative judgment being made against those who disagree about "taking the Bible literally," I have found that the most effective way to get a discussion started is to make biblical literalists prove that they really do take the Bible literally. You begin by quoting a series like: "Come, let us sing joyfully to the LORD; let us acclaim the Rock of our salvation" (Ps 95:1); "I am the light of the world" (John 8:12); and "Whoever comes to me will never hunger, and whoever believes in me will never thirst" (John 6:35). Then you ask whether God really is a rock, whether Jesus actually traveled at 300,000 kilometers per second—the speed of light—on his journeys in Palestine, and whether Christians ever have experienced hunger or thirst. As soon as biblical "literalists" admit that some statements must be understood in a figurative sense, one has to ask how they know which ones these are.

After many years of reading and studying the Bible, I wish that I knew, for sure, all the biblical passages that are meant to be taken literally, all the parts that have a different sort of meaning, and how to interpret these various sections. But I do not know, and even more to the point, I do not believe that other Christians know either. Finally, I do not see that it is fair for Christian folks who disagree with other Christian folks to say that anyone who disagrees with them cannot be saved, especially when they are unable to provide either a logical explanation or some miraculous event to substantiate a claim to supernatural revelation.

In the rest of this book we shall explore some of the literary clues in the Bible that can help us decide what pericopes were intended to be read in a "literal" sense and which have some other kind of meaning. Although many literal facts can be discovered in the Bible, the Bible is not a book filled with facts. It is a book filled with history, proverbs, parables, sermons, letters, poems, hymns, and so on. And unless we know something about those genres, we can never understand the Scriptures.

CHAPTER 2

Parables

Probably the easiest genre to recognize in the Bible is that of the parable. The most familiar parables are those Jesus told. They are easier to find than examples of other genres because the gospel writers often introduce a parable by calling it a parable.

Knowing that a biblical passage is a parable, however, does not necessarily give us a direct understanding of what the message of the parable is. The major problem for modern readers is that the biblical authors never spelled out the complete procedure for interpreting parables. A few parables have explanations added, but most stand by themselves. That means we have to work inductively when we study parables. We do that by reading the biblical passages called parables and looking for what they might have in common with other parables as we attempt to interpret them.

Because the biblical authors *recorded* parables but did not *explain* the literary nature of parables, later readers have tried to understand the genre as best they could. Parables have been defined in a number of ways. A modern reader can find parables described as stories or statements that (1) compare something common with something uncommon, (2) attempt to make a single major point about correct behavior, (3) help people think about a complex issue by providing an illustration that puts the issue into the context of everyday life, or (4) convey a message to the wise that will be misunderstood by the simple.

Trying to define the exact nature of parables is beyond our present study. This book is not meant to resolve ongoing technical debates among scholars. But, even if we cannot know as much as we would like to, it is still possible to know a great deal about parables without knowing everything about them. What I want to do in this chapter is give some general guidelines about discovering and interpreting parables.

The easiest way to find parables is to look for the passages that are actually called parables in the text. Matthew 13:31 provides an example of this external contextual evidence about genre: "He proposed another parable to them. 'The kingdom of heaven is like a mustard seed that a person took and sowed in a field . . .'"

Many parables, however, must be identified on the basis of internal evidence. In Luke 14:16-17 Jesus begins the parable of the wedding feast by saying: "A man gave a great dinner to which he invited many. When the time for the dinner came, he dispatched his servant to say to those invited, 'Come, everything is now ready.'" Even though Jesus mentioned this "man," he was not intending for us to believe that there really had been such a man. Instead, he was using one of the standard introductory phrases for parables. Also used in other parables are phrases like "There was a man . . ." or "There was a woman . . ."

We give similiar literary clues when we introduce fairy tales by saying, "Once upon a time . . ." No one who hears that introductory phrase to the story of Cinderella, except perhaps for some small child, thinks that the speaker intends us to believe that there actually is either a date that we can associate with Cinderella, say A.D. 1207, or a specific location, say on the eastern edge of the Black Forest, where she was so mistreated by her stepsisters. The introductory phrase is the clue that we are going to hear a fairy tale. And, just as fairy tales usually have some sort of moral that one discovers after hearing the story, parables also make some point that could not be as easily communicated except by the story or illustration they provide.

Many parables do not begin by mentioning "a woman" or "a man." Their introductory clue is a question about something complex, which is then answered by an illustration coming out of everyday life. An example of this is Jesus' parable of the yeast in Luke 13:20-21: "Again he said, 'To what shall I compare the kingdom of God? It is like yeast that a woman took and mixed [in] with three measures of wheat flour until the whole batch of dough was leavened.'"

But recognizing parables is neither very difficult nor very inspiring. It is only the first step. The real challenge of reading parables is making sense of them. Since they were never meant to be taken literally, we have to search for the nonliteral meaning hidden inside. Let us consider Matthew 13:45-46, the parable of the pearl, as an example. " 'Again, the kingdom of heaven is like a merchant searching for fine pearls. When he finds a pearl of great price, he goes and sells all that he has and buys it.' "

Understanding this parable requires using imagination and intuition. To discover the point we need to think about the pericope as a whole. For someone who takes the Bible literally but who ignores the literary nature of the material, this parable will not make much sense. After all, Jesus is not saying that since the kingdom of heaven is like a merchant, it normally has a temperature of 98.6 degrees Fahrenheit, or that it goes to sleep at night, or that it is always interested in making a good profit on its investments. Instead Jesus is making a point about what a person should do when he or she discovers a treasure of incredible worth. One needs to be willing to give up those other things that once mattered in order to possess the newly found treasure.

The key to understanding parables is searching for the primary message of the parable as a whole.

The most common error in reading parables is looking for too many messages. Or, to put it into more specific language, the most common error in reading parables is to assume that they are allegories. Allegories are fictional narratives in which each major person, place, thing, or action in the story is meant to stand for something else in the real world. Modern examples of allegories are John Bunyan's *Pilgrim's Progress* and C. S. Lewis *The Pilgrim's Regress*. There are a number of allegories in the Bible, especially in Revelation. For example, the scarlet woman in Revelation 17 and the various items associated with her were intended to represent individuals and incidents from the persecutions that Christians were suffering at the hands of the Roman Empire in the first century.

Nevertheless, there are a few parables that *are* given allegorical interpretations in the Bible. The parable of the sower, for example, in Mark 4:1-9 is interpreted somewhat allegorically by Jesus. He explains that the seed sown represents the word of God, the seed that falls on the rocky soil represents those who hear the word gladly, the weeds represent the cares of this world, and so on. But, even though this parable is written in a sort of code, the parable of the sower still has the overall point that different people will respond differently to the word of God.

Almost all of the other parables seem not to need this extended allegorical interpretation. They only try to make one major point. The problem with using allegorical interpretations is trying to make the parables too relevant to contemporary situations. This can lead to ridiculous interpretations. For example, if one explained the parable of the sower by saying that the seed represented television evangelism, the seed on the rocky soil represented people who switch channels too often, and the weeds represented commercial television, we would be quite justified in saying that Jesus intended no such meaning when he used this parable.

Understanding allegories involves solving the puzzle or, to describe it better, breaking the code. One discovers what the allegory is about and then figures out what the various items are meant to stand for. But there is no real check on this method of interpretation once a person starts it. He or she can project almost any meaning desired into the passage being studied. It is much better to focus on finding the primary meaning of the parable rather than letting your imagination run wild.

Another major problem in understanding parables also involves ignoring the primary meaning of the passage. But, in contrast to misreading parables as allegories, with this error one does not break the allegorical code but instead assumes that the major character involved is showing behavior we are to imitate. Of course, in the parable of the pearl and the parable of the woman and the lost coin (Luke 15:8-10), we could legitimately imitate the behavior of the major characters. But in other parables major characters act in ways that are surely inappropriate for Christians. Consider the parable of the unjust steward (Luke 16:1-8). Jesus tells of a rich man who audited the steward who managed his property and, when he found that his steward was cheating on the accounts, gave the man a bonus because he had been so clever with his finagling. I do not believe that Jesus intended for us to follow the example of either the rich man or the steward. His point was, as near as I can tell, that many people are clever when it comes to scheming at ways to make money but foolish when it comes to considering what is really important.

The parable is showing that the behavior of both rich man and steward was shortsighted.

Even though parables often reveal something about how people are to act, sometimes the parable as a whole is meant to cause an emotional reaction that leads to an action not described in the parable. In 2 Samuel 12:1-4, Nathan the prophet tells a parable to King David about a rich man who stole a lamb, a beloved pet, from a poor man in their village and used the slaughtered lamb as the main course at the rich man's banquet. The prophet intended for the parable to inflame and anger the king. David was hooked by the story and was angered by the rich man's behavior, a callous abuse of power, which David then wanted to punish. When David demanded to know the rich man's name, Nathan stated (2 Sam 12:7), "You are the man!" The parable described an unjust act that was similar to the abuse of power David had committed when he arranged for the murder of Uriah so that David could marry Uriah's widow. The parable was meant to evoke a feeling, and that feeling was supposed to lead to action.

Although there are many different reasons given for people speaking in parables, Matthew 13:10-17 states that parables are meant to reveal mysteries. But mysteries are mysterious. And modern readers going through the parables may find themselves disagreeing about what a parable is really saying. That is both the strength and the weakness of parables. They are very good at communicating a feeling or helping you see something from a new angle. But it can be very difficult to explain feelings and images. I think it is possible that Jesus chose to use parables so often because he himself was aware that some truths are better expressed in stories than in logical exposition.

CHAPTER 3

Proverbs

Proverbs are sayings that give advice about behavior. There is no problem coming up with examples of them: "A stitch in time saves nine," "Loose lips sink ships," "Don't look a gift horse in the mouth." Since there is a book in the Bible called Proverbs, as well as isolated proverbs sprinkled throughout the other books, it is important that we come to an understanding of how to interpret them.

The proverbs we can find in the Bible are a mixed bag. They range from the profound Proverbs 21:13, "He who shuts his ear to the cry of the poor will himself also call and not be heard," to the rather gossipy Titus 1:12, "Cretans have always been liars, vicious beasts, and lazy gluttons." When we look at a proverb, we sometimes need to balance what it is saying with some other proverb. For example, compare Proverbs 20:1, "Wine is arrogant, strong drink is riotous; none who goes astray for it is wise," with 1 Timothy 5:23, "Stop drinking only water, but have a little wine for the sake of your stomach and your frequent illnesses."

When we begin to interpret proverbs, the first thing to notice is that although proverbs give advice about behavior, they are often in the form of statements and not in the form of commands. The advice about how to behave in these cases is not stated but rather implied by the proverb. For example, if someone wanted to follow a modern proverb literally, how should that person interpret

"Loose lips sink ships"? Is it enough to say that he or she believes the proverb to be true? But the point of this proverb is not to provide an explanation of why ships sink. Ships sink for all sorts of reasons. The message of this proverb is not stated explicitly but instead is implied. It gives a warning to keep quiet about information that others might use against you.

The second thing to notice about proverbs is that no one with sense takes them literally. Understanding proverbs requires the reader or listener to go beyond the simple advice implied by the proverb and to apply the message in a different context. "A stitch in time saves nine" is not just meant to advise people about sewing up small rips in clothing. The proverb is giving advice about the importance of looking after small problems before they turn into big problems.

Understanding proverbs requires wisdom. We have to figure out what the message of the proverb is, see what it might apply to in our lives, and then decide if the advice really applies to us at the present time. That last suggestion is important because proverbs are often contradictory. Consider two well known nonbiblical proverbs, "Look before you leap" and "He who hesitates is lost." A person hearing these two proverbs might conclude that they contradict each other and deny that there is any value in them. But is that the right way to understand them?

Does not each of these proverbs give good advice? I think that each proverb is full of useful and important advice. But what requires wisdom on our part is figuring out under what circumstances each one applies. At times in my life I needed to hear "He who hesitates is lost." At other times I needed to consider "Look before you leap." Neither proverb was meant as a guide for all human life at all times. Someone with wisdom will recognize the value of particular proverbs depending on the circumstances that he or she is in.

These general comments help explain some of the "contradictions" one can find among the proverbs of the Bible. Consider the two which occur side by side in Proverbs 26:4-5:

> Answer not the fool according to his folly,
>   lest you too become like him.
> Answer the fool according to his folly,
>   lest he become wise in his own eyes.

Considering this issue on a strictly biblical basis, how is someone supposed to answer a fool? Do you speak foolishly along with him or do you reply in a serious manner? Even though a literal reading of these proverbs will cause them to be seen in contradiction, I do not see them in that way. It seems to me that in understanding proverbs, an intelligent woman must judge whether the advice applies to her own situation. Does she want to make the foolish person get serious? Or is she willing to kid along with the foolish person because the other person is presently incapable of being serious? In either case the Bible is giving good advice. The challenge is discovering if and when it applies.

In the New Testament Jesus says a number of proverbs. In the Sermon on the Mount he states two with a similar meaning (Matt 7:6). "Do not give what is holy to dogs, or throw your pearls before swine, lest they trample them under foot, and turn and tear you to pieces." Just what does he mean? I am not entirely sure what specifically Jesus had in mind. Obviously he is not talking about giving Communion wafers to, say, Snoopy or about tossing the crown jewels in front of the trough at the pig farm.

Understanding this proverb requires that we figure out what is holy and who the swine are. There are a number of things I can think of that are regularly called holy: the Holy Bible, the Holy Eucharist, the Holy Father, holy matrimony. And there are a number of things that are in fact holy but not necessarily called holy in everyday speech: the Gospel, the Creeds, the Twelve Apostles, and so on.

Perhaps the proverb's message here is a warning not to give something sacred to people who will not be able to appreciate it. But I think it would be taking this proverb too far to say that Christians are not to share the gospel with nonbelievers since it is a holy thing and nonbelievers will not appreciate it. All in all, understanding Matthew 7:6 means seeing that it applies to some situations, but not all possible situations, and that a man or woman must use wisdom to discover when it applies in his or her life. All of us, at one time or another, have to deal with pearls (or swine), and we need to think about our behavior with them.

Easier to understand is Jesus' proverb in Matthew 5:14, "A city set on a mountain cannot be hidden." Jesus is not teaching us about geography or camouflage in this statement but is pointing out that important things cannot be hidden. The sentences before and after this proverb show that he intended it to apply to his followers. They are to be the light of the world and to shine their light throughout the world so that all might give praise to the Father in heaven. Jesus' proverb here is probably easier to interpret than the one about pearls and swine, because this one has a more general application.

The basic rules for interpreting proverbs involve recognizing that the pericope one is reading is a proverb, discovering its message, seeing how that message might apply to our lives, and then deciding if (or when) it gives advice we need to take. That last step requires not only being open to the biblical text but also being aware enough of ourselves to know that the advice we need to hear is not always the advice we want to hear.

Finally, quoting biblical proverbs to other people can be just as risky as quoting any other Bible passage. Unless we have thought very seriously about the application of a proverb to another person's situation, we may do more harm than good. As Proverbs 26:9 expresses it, "Like a thorn stick brandished by the hand of a drunkard is a proverb in the mouth of fools." The fool quoting proverbs is just as likely to harm others (and himself) as is the drunkard who is waving around a branch with thorns.

CHAPTER 4

Promises

There are many promises in the Bible. Jesus, Paul, Moses, and the prophets not only make their own promises but also tell of promises being made to others by God. The major problem modern readers have with interpreting biblical promises is not so much finding them but figuring out when and to whom they apply.

In Hebrews 13:5 the author quotes God giving the promise "I will never forsake you or abandon you." In this last chapter of Hebrews the author is summing up much of what he had said earlier and is giving advice about how people are to behave. The promise he quotes is actually a rewording of the affirmation found in Deuteronomy 31:6 near the end of Moses' sermon there: "He will never fail you or forsake you." Since this affirmation is found in both the Old and New Testaments, is in a variety of texts, and seems addressed to two general audiences, I believe that it is a promise that still applies to believers today.

Yet this promise, like so many others in the Bible, would be very easy to misinterpret. One must note the specifics of the promise. God's presence is promised to us, but that does not necessarily mean that we will always feel it. Perhaps this promise also functions as a reminder that even when we feel ourselves absolutely alone and isolated, God is still with us. In addition, the promise makes no claim that only good things are going to happen to us because of God's presence.

In contrast to this general promise, there are other biblical promises that seem to be more limited in scope. In the book of

Deuteronomy we can find dozens of other promises in Moses' sermon. How are we to interpret them? Consider the rather general promises of growth and prosperity made in Deuteronomy 6:3. "Hear then, Israel, and be careful to observe [God's statutes and commandments], that you may grow and prosper the more, in keeping with the promise of the LORD, the God of your fathers, to give you a land flowing with milk and honey."

But God's promises can be much more specific, as in Deuteronomy 7:12-14.

> As your reward for heeding these decrees and observing them carefully, the LORD, your God, will keep with you the merciful covenant which he promised on oath to your fathers. He will love and bless and multiply you; he will bless the fruit of your womb and the produce of your soil, your grain and wine and oil, the issue of your herds and the young of your flocks, in the land which he swore to your fathers he would give you. You will be blessed above all peoples; no man or woman among you shall be childless nor shall your livestock be barren.

Were these promises meant only for the Israelites who followed Moses into the Promised Land, or are they meant for Christians today? As much as someone who owned a ranch might like to take Deuteronomy 7:13-14 as God's personal promise about livestock production, verse 12 sets the condition that the recipients of the promise are to observe the laws that had been given to them. Further, the audience being addressed in Deuteronomy is a nation over three thousand years ago and not an individual reader today.

How can modern believers know if a biblical promise is meant to apply to individuals today? And how can we know if a promise made to one group, say to the ancient nation of Israel, can apply to another group today, say to the modern nation of Brazil or to those folks who happen to live in northeast Minneapolis?

A necessary step in interpreting promises found in the Bible is admitting that many of the promises recorded were not meant for all people at all times. For one thing, many promises are conditional ones. If Israel or some particular person does something, then the promise will be fulfilled. Secondly and more importantly, many promises seem obviously restricted to specific times, places, and people. If every promise found in the Bible were meant to be applied universally, then most of them would have been proven false.

I prefer to think that we have misinterpreted a biblical text by applying it too broadly rather than to think that God had lied.

Consider two promises that appear to have been limited to specific times and people. In Genesis 28:13-15, Jacob is having a dream in which he sees a ladder going up into heaven from the earth:

> And there was the LORD standing beside him and saying: "I, the LORD, am the God of your forefather Abraham and the God of Isaac; the land on which you are lying I will give to you and your descendants. These shall be as plentiful as the dust of the earth, and through them you shall spread out east and west, north and south. In you and your descendants all the nations of the earth shall find blessing. Know that I am with you; I will protect you wherever you go, and bring you back to this land. I will never leave you until I have done what I promised you."

The promises made here appear to be meant for Jacob and his descendants. But similarly specific promises can also be found in the New Testament. In Matthew 9:19-22 there is a narrative that tells of Jesus healing a women who touched him. She seems to have been afraid to speak to Jesus directly and so slips beside him and touches his cloak. "Jesus turned and saw her, and said, 'Courage, daughter! Your faith has saved you.' And from that hour the woman was cured."

As much as I would like to think that having faith would cause a person to be healed of any disease, Jesus' promise here appears to be specifically limited to the woman who touched him. Note that this promise is recorded in a narrative that tells of a personal encounter between Jesus and the woman. Jesus did not make this promise to a general audience in a sermon or to a group of people receiving a letter.

After seeing that many promises recorded in the Bible are conditional or were meant for specific people in different circumstances, we can consider what is probably the most common error in interpreting this genre: "claiming promises." This claiming of promises involves reading the Bible, finding something you feel speaks to you, and then believing that it directly applies to you as God's personal promise.

There is something odd about this whole approach to reading the Bible. For example, imagine a college student, Sharon, who is disappointed with the grade she has received on a term paper. She expresses her concern to the professor of the course. The professor knows Sharon and is aware of her other grades. The professor then says: "Don't worry about the grade on your term paper. Because of all your other excellent work, you'll still get an *A* in the course." Now imagine that on the next day another student in the class, Bob, comes up to the professor and says: "Thanks for your promise, Dr. Jones. I'm so glad you said, 'Don't worry about the grade on your term paper. You'll still get an *A* in the course.' Thanks for promising that I'll get an *A*." I think the professor would have good grounds to object to Bob's claiming the promise made to Sharon. The promise was for her, not for Bob. Even though Bob has quoted Dr. Jones exactly, it would still be unfair of Bob to accuse the professor of being dishonest. A person does not have the right to "claim" promises that were made to other people.

This is not to say that we should never believe that certain promises are meant for us. A person might be led by the Holy Spirit to believe that a promise originally made to King David could apply to her or him now. But the ultimate basis of that belief is a personal feeling, which may or may not be correct. And just as our feelings may accurately reflect the influence of the Holy Spirit, they may also sometimes reflect what we wish was the influence of the Holy Spirit. A personal conviction about the present applicability of a promise cannot be based upon reading the Bible as a thousand-page contract in which the Party of the First Part (God) promises to do certain things for the party of the second part (me) whenever the latter party points out those promises to the Party of the First Part and says, "But you promised."

Yet there are promises that continue to be difficult to interpret. Consider John 15:7, part of the farewell speech Jesus makes to his disciples before he is arrested, "If you remain in me and my words remain in you, ask for whatever you want and it will be done for you." Was this promise meant only for the disciples gathered around the table with Jesus or is there a broader group (including us today) for whom the promise is being made?

I am inclined to believe that this promise has a broader application. But that judgment is based on the fact that there are several important qualifications stated before the promise. One qualification is to be in Christ and have his words in one's heart. Jesus was not making a simple promise that we can get whatever we want just by asking for it. His promise was based on the assumption that those who are in Christ will not only know how to ask but will also know about what they should ask. In other words, I may not get a new sports car just because I ask for it.

There is no foolproof way to interpret promises in the Bible. Like everyone else, I want a number of very specific good things to happen to me and to my loved ones. And more than once, I, too, have been tempted to claim promises made to others.

Probably the best check on this sort of self-centered interpretation of the Bible is to study the Scriptures in a group, especially in a group of people who do not all think alike. By being in such a group, one can hear the thoughts and experiences others have had. By studying together we can also discover to what extent we may inappropriately be claiming promises and whether we are really being open to God's word.

CHAPTER 5

Hymns

Jewish and Christian congregations have been singing hymns for thousands of years. The most familiar biblical examples of hymns can be found in the Book of Psalms. Although some psalms were probably composed as individual works of personal meditation, the majority of the psalms were hymns, which believers chanted or sang as a group. But hymns are not confined to the psalms. In the Old Testament they can also be found in the Song of Solomon, which is also called the Song of Songs in some Bibles, and in Exodus 15. In addition, most scholars have concluded that there is at least one hymn in the New Testament. (Paul's *quotation* of that hymn will be examined in another chapter.)

In thinking about how to interpret hymns, we can begin by considering why people sing hymns. Most of us sing because we enjoy it. My voice has never been good, but I still enjoy being able to join in a congregation's singing, especially when there are stronger voices giving me help in keeping up with the beat and following the melody. Singing can be enjoyable in itself, and experiencing the sound and community spirit of a crowd singing together is for many people the high point of worshiping. When congregations sing together, there is an increase in group solidarity.

Singing means sharing something of ourselves. And very often we are reminded of other people and places as well. Many memories from our personal past can be evoked during congregational singing. The memories need not be conscious pictures or words. Sometimes we experience only a brief wave of old feelings and emotions.

I think that explains why so many people do not like new hymns in worship services. Their opportunity to relive personal history is taken away. Yet hymns can also remind us of the history we share with other believers, and no selection of hymns will ever meet everyone's expectations.

The primary distinction to keep in mind when we read hymns in the Bible is that a hymn is not a creed. Even though there are some Churches that might sing the Nicene Creed or some other statement of faith, in general we sing hymns for a different reason than we recite creeds. Creeds were meant to summarize as accurately as possible what Christians believe (or once believed). The typical procedure was for creeds to be composed by groups of believers who discussed every word that appeared in the statements. Every word, phrase, and idea was put there for a reason that seemed important at the time. This method of composition is in radical contrast to that of hymns. The words, phrases, and ideas in hymns are usually the composition of an individual, and they typically express a more personal interpretation of life and faith.

The conclusion to be drawn from looking at these different methods of compositions in reference to modern hymns is that we should look upon biblical hymns in the same manner. The psalms, for example, are not necessarily creeds or teachings. Most of them express the individual feelings of their authors. Sometimes, but by no means always, we can affirm the feelings of the authors. Consider, for example, Psalm 58:7-11.

> O God, smash their teeth in their mouths;
>   the jaw-teeth of the lions, break, O LORD!
> Let them vanish like water flowing off;
>   when they draw the bow, let their arrows be headless shafts.
> Let them dissolve like a melting snail,
>   like an untimely birth that never sees the sun.
> Unexpectedly, like a thorn bush,
>   or like thistles, let the whirlwind carry them away.
> The just man shall be glad when he sees vengeance;
>   he shall bathe his feet in the blood of the wicked.
> And men shall say, "Truly there is a reward for the just;
>   truly there is a God who is judge on earth."

The last stanza suggests that the righteous will be able to look upon washing their feet in the blood of the wicked as a reward for their own goodness. It will be an activity to rejoice in. In order to understand these verses, we need to recognize that the Bible is not teaching that we should bathe our feet in other people's blood or that this activity is being promised as a reward to us. Rather these stanzas express the emotional outrage the ancient author felt because of the wicked who abused their power. The reasons for his feelings can be seen in the earlier verses, Psalm 58:2-6.

> Do you indeed like gods pronounce justice
>   and judge fairly, you men of rank?
> Nay, you willingly commit crimes;
>   on earth you look to the fruits of extortion.
> From the womb the wicked are perverted;
>   astray from birth have the liars gone.
> Theirs is poison like a serpent's,
>   like that of a stubborn snake that stops its ears,
> That it may not hear the voice of enchanters
>   casting cunning spells.

I do not think that modern Christians need share the author's particular desire for revenge, but we can share the feelings of outrage he felt for dishonest judges in positions of power. And, given that we recognize that ancient society had different views of violence and revenge than we do now, we can also—to some extent—understand why he wanted to see the blood of his enemies. (Now that our civilization is so advanced, we prefer death and destruction to be carried out from a more distant vantage point. That is why we prefer bombs and chemical weapons to swords and spears.)

Further, just as we need not share in all the personal desires expressed in biblical hymns, I do not see that we need accept all the theological, scientific, medical, political, or anthropological implications of the hymns. For example, consider the theological implications of Psalm 13:2.

> How long, O Lord? Will you utterly forget me?
> How long will you hide your face from me?

In this verse the author is expressing his feelings of isolation. He is not teaching that God has the sort of mind that forgets things or that God actually has a face that could be hidden.

Neither are hymns meant to teach us about science. Rather they demonstrate the scientific understandings of their authors. Psalm

24:1-2, for example, is not a direct challenge to the modern geological theory of plate techtonics.

> The LORD's are the earth and its fullness;
>   the world and those who dwell in it.
> For he founded it upon the seas
>   and established it upon the rivers.

In this psalm, the author shows his familiarity with the ancient view that the earth floats upon the waters of the deep. He is not presenting the Bible's view of continental foundations. It would require a total misunderstanding of the genre of hymns to imagine that Christians are required to object to plate techtonics because that modern theory goes against the Bible's teaching that land masses are supported by water.

In addition, surely no one would argue that Christians are to withhold medical treatment for the elderly even though Psalm 90:10 affirms,

> Seventy is the sum of our years,
>   or eighty, if we are strong.

The author is giving a lament that life is so short. He is not teaching us about the maximum length of life allowable for believers. He is not telling us to pull the plug on anyone over eighty.

In the same manner, the political implications of the psalms (if they were interpreted as teachings about how government and society should operate) would be that slavery was the natural order of things and that rule by kings and royal families was preferable to other political systems. Kings and royal families were part of the world order in biblical times. They appear in the psalms because they were part of the ancient world and not necessarily because God wants us to scrap the democratic process.

Finally, the anthropological implications about human nature in the psalms are reflective of the author's individual views and may or may not indicate what the Christian position ought to be. Consider the description of humanity in Psalm 14:1b-3.

> There is not one who does good.
> The LORD looks down from heaven
>   upon the children of men,
>   to see if there be one who is wise and seeks God.

> All alike have gone astray; they have become perverse;
> there is not one who does good, not even one.

Are modern Christians to look upon this portion of the psalm as a summation of the biblical view of human nature, or should we consider this as a statement of the author's feelings of betrayal and disillusionment?

When we come to an understanding of how the genre of hymns must influence our interpretation of them, we should be alert to the danger of overinterpreting what we find in them. But once we admit that the hymns of the Bible primarily reflect the thoughts and feelings of earlier individuals, we must also be aware of the possibility that the theological (or social or anthropological) implications in them might indeed reflect biblical teaching. I do not believe that modern Christians have the right simply to reject whatever they do not like in the hymns. But neither should we accept recorded personal meditation as biblical teaching. In order to avoid these two extremes and discover how the Bible is relevant now, we must interpret the hymns by drawing out their implications and then comparing the individual author's insights with what we find elsewhere in the Bible.

CHAPTER 6

Narratives

Narratives are found throughout the Bible. Genesis begins with a narrative about the creation of the world, and the last chapter in Revelation contains the end of a narrative in which the author describes the vision of heaven he has experienced. A narrative is, to put it very simply, a story. There will be a character or characters in the story, and they will either do something or have something happen to them.

As you can probably tell from that last sentence, the literary category of narrative is a very wide genre. It actually serves as the general term for a number of more specific genres. In fact, knowing that a Biblical passage is a narrative does not help us very much when we attempt to understand it. What we really need to know is whether the narrative being studied is a parable, a history, a myth, a legend, an epic, a joke, a short story, or something else. I am not saying that all of these types of narratives can be found within the Bible, but they do illustrate the range of possibilities along which narratives can be more accurately classified.

It is only after we get a better idea of the specific genre we are reading that we can begin to interpret the narrative at hand. When we find a Biblical passage that tells a story, we must look for the internal and external clues that will tell us what sort of narrative we are reading. In an earlier chapter we considered the internal and external clues that indicate that a given narrative is a parable. In later chapters we will explore three other types of narratives (history, legend, and myth), which can be found on the pages between Genesis and Revelation.

The most common mistake in reading a narrative is taking a part of it out of context. By that I mean focusing on a few words or a few verses within the narrative and ignoring the point of the narrative as a whole. For example, imagine a contemporary man reading a newspaper story about the financial success of a millionaire who has made his millions by purchasing shares of stock in IBM. The man reading the newspaper is wondering what to do with his savings account and decides to turn to the Bible for help. He lets the Bible fall open, and his eyes fall upon Luke 10:37, where he reads the sentence, "Jesus said to him, 'Go and do likewise.' " The newspaper reader decides that God is telling him to invest in IBM.

As far as I know, I do not have anything against people who read newspapers or people who invest in IBM, but I do think that the newspaper reader in this illustration has made two major errors in his decision to buy IBM stocks. His most serious mistake is "bibliomancy," that is, using a randomly selected passage from the Bible for the purpose of divination. In other words, he is seeking guidance about the future by using the Bible as a fortunetelling device.

Less superstitious but equally foolish is his second mistake, taking Luke 10:37 out of its context. This sentence is the final comment in the pericope in which Jesus tells the parable of the Good Samaritan. The narrative involved here begins at Luke 10:25. And the point of Jesus telling the parable and following it with the exhortation "Go and do likewise" seems to be that we are to follow the example of the Good Samaritan by helping people in need. The newspaper reader has missed the whole point. IBM might be a good stock to invest in, but our investor will have to discover its potential in some other fashion.

The misinterpretation of narratives is not limited to the sort of frivolous example provided above. An overly emotional state or a period of great stress can often overwhelm any ability to hear the wisdom contained in the Bible. As an example of this, consider a seriously ill woman reading the narrative about Adam and Eve in the Garden of Eden (Gen 3:1-24). In the story of the Fall the serpent clinches his temptation of Eve by saying, "You certainly will not die." The sick woman begins to think about that sentence while she is in the hospital.

There are two different ways of misinterpreting the serpent's statement to Eve, either one of which could lead to the seriously

ill woman causing harm to those she loves. The first possibility is
that she might decide that she does not need to make a will because God is telling her *by this verse* that she is going to live. The
second possibility is just the opposite. The woman might conclude
that since the serpent had been lying when he said, "You will not
die," she needs to give up any idea of living because God is telling
her *by this verse* that she is going to die. The potential harm that
the ill woman might cause to others is based, to some extent, on
a misguided reading of Genesis 3. My own opinion is that the seriously ill woman would do better to speak with and to listen to
her physician, her pastor, her friends, her family, and her own self
as she attempts to come to terms with her illness. Becoming ob-
sessed with isolated Bible verses seldom does any good. And ex-
pecting a direct communication from God just because you read
the Bible seems to be turning God into an all-loving "gofer."

By saying that, I do not mean to imply that Christians should
never have any feelings of assurance or that any belief about God
communicating directly with someone is false. Such things are possible. But the personal conviction of those feelings and beliefs develops from a subjective experience. One cannot claim that they
are based in some objective reality found in the Bible. Biblical narratives can indeed speak to us, but many of them are stories that
simply do not apply to our present individual circumstances. To
discover what narratives might be relevant to our personal circumstances requires studying and reading the Bible on a more serious
level than merely dropping it on the table as a way of letting it fall
open to "the verse of the day."

After figuring out what kind of narrative one is reading, the next
most crucial factor is keeping in mind that the narrative as a whole
needs to direct how the individual parts of it are to be interpreted.

This can sometimes be more of a challenge than at first appears.
For, even though short and straightforward narratives tell a simple
story, longer narratives can be much more complicated. In longer
narratives we can find dialogues, soliloquies, prayers, promises, lies,
half-truths, parables, proverbs, sermons, laws, and on and on. These
get included in the narratives because these things are happening
among the characters. There can be genres within other genres.

This idea of overlapping genres is not hard to grasp. Throughout nonbiblical literature one can find novels, for example, that

also contain poems, lectures, sermons, songs, parables, and even short stories. There can be narratives within narratives. Within the Bible, larger narratives would be entire books like Exodus, the Gospels, or Esther. And within these larger narratives we can find shorter narratives, as well as other genres such as sermons, laws, or promises.

The key point, though, is that one must consider the narrative as a whole before one makes a final conclusion on what any given part of it means. This policy serves to guard against making major mistakes, like taking the serpent's lie as a direct communication from God or ignoring the overall effect of a story by limiting our focus to a single verse.

Making sense of complex narratives is a two-way street. In one direction, you move from the narrative as a whole to the individual components. In the other direction, you move from individual pericopes to the narrative as a whole. Both directions are important.

The Gospel According to Matthew is a very complex narrative and will illustrate this dual process. In order to understand a major portion of that narrative, say, the Sermon on the Mount (Matt 5–7), one must consider how the sermon fits in with the overall narrative of the Gospel. For example, does Matthew present Jesus in such a way that we might be justified in thinking that Jesus is being ironic when he delivered the Sermon on the Mount? To be more specific, when Jesus is quoted in Matthew 5:5 saying, "Blessed are the meek, for they will inherit the land," is he being sarcastic?

Even though a skilled actor could read the Sermon on the Mount to an audience with a sarcastic tone in his voice, even to the point of making the audience believe that the sermon was meant ironically, I do not believe that anyone who has read the whole of Matthew would ever be convinced by such a perverse interpretation of the smaller part.

That is one direction in the dual process. The other direction involves making sense of Matthew's Gospel as a complete narrative. To acquire a holistic view of the work, we must read the individual literary components: parables, proverbs, quotations, dialogues, sermons, miracle narratives, genealogy, passion narrative, resurrection narrative, and so on. Then, on the basis of all this material in all these different genres, we develop an opinion on what Matthew was trying to tell us when he wrote his entire Gospel.

The opinion we reach may be a profound and convincing interpretation (like a judge's opinion on a matter of law). But the power of a particular interpretation is in its ability to make sense out of all the individual components in Matthew. So if our opinion of Matthew's purpose in writing the Gospel involves ignoring substantial portions of the text or rejecting the message of individual pericopes because they seem to contradict one another, we probably need to hold that opinion more tentatively.

CHAPTER 7

Letters

Most of the books in the New Testament are letters. Knowing that a text is a letter, however, does not necessarily tell us very much about how to interpret it. Letters, whether ancient or modern, come in many different forms. And, unless we know the kind of letter we are reading, we are likely to stumble into the sort of error illustrated by the man who read the phone book as if it were a novel.

To help us begin this examination of biblical letters, I want to point out how diverse the modern genre of letters is. There are love letters and "Dear John" letters, letters of introduction and letters of resignation, family letters and thank-you letters. The mail we get can range between junk mail and fan mail. But the possibilities are not exhausted by these sorts of letters addressed to individuals. On a more formal level, one can think of a "letter of protest," which one government might send another, a "letter of agreement" between corporations, or a "pastoral letter," which a group of bishops could send to members of a Church. For example, the Roman Catholic bishops in America wrote a pastoral letter on the economy in the 1980s.

Even though we can usually tell what kind of letter we are reading within a sentence or two in the first paragraph, many modern letters are deliberately written so that they will mislead their readers. Almost everyone has received a letter which starts out with a "Dear Friend" and turns out to be a form letter from some business you have never heard of. The main problem we encounter in making sense of biblical letters, however, does not develop because they were written to mislead us but because we do not always take account of why the particular letter was written.

When we think about why letters are written, we need to go beyond the simplistic explanation that all letters are meant to convey information to those who are far away. While it is probably true that all letters, whether ancient or modern, convey some information, that is seldom the primary purpose that underlies a given letter. The primary purpose of many letters is to express some affection (such as love, friendship, sympathy, gratitude, congratulations, and so on). But letters can also give orders, make threats, encourage people to "keep up the good work," or attempt to persuade the recipients to do something.

Further, in most letters longer than a paragraph or so, there are usually a number of purposes that motivated the author to write. For example, college students regularly write letters which not only convey information about their studies but which also request an extra forty dollars for long distance telephone calls. Or, as another modern example, a love letter might also attempt to persuade the recipient to come out for a weekend visit.

Similar combinations of purposes for writing also underlie biblical letters. Consider Paul's Letter to the Philippians. Paul expresses affection for them throughout the letter. What he says in Philippians 1:7 about his love can serve as an illustration of this pattern: "It is right that I should think this way about all of you, because I hold you in my heart, you who are all partners with me in grace, both in my imprisonment and in the defense and confirmation of the gospel." There are over twenty sentences, phrases, or words by which Paul refers to the feelings of love and gratitude he has toward the Philippians. In addition, Paul provides some information in chapter 2 about his assistant Timothy and the messenger Epaphroditus, whom the Philippians had sent to him, and near the end of the letter he reminds the Philippians of the partnership they share with him in his missionary work.

As important as these biographical elements and expressions of affection are for showing us what kind of man Paul was, I do not believe that they reveal the primary motivation Paul had for writing this particular letter. Throughout the letter Paul attempts to encourage his readers to persevere in the Christian life. In Philippians 1:27 he puts it this way: "Only, conduct yourselves in a way worthy of the gospel of Christ, so that, whether I come and see you or am absent, I may hear news of you, that you are standing firm in one spirit. . . ." In addition to this somewhat general exhortation to the Christian life (and others, which can be found in Phil 2:12-13; 3:1, 15, etc.), Paul can also get quite specific about how Christians are to behave. He urges the Philippians to act with selflessness and without grumbling. He even makes the outrageous exhortation that the Philippians should not only follow him in what he *says* but also follow him in what he *does* (3:17 and 4:9).

There is a technical word for the type of letter illustrated by Philippians. It and most of the other New Testament letters are "paranetic" letters. There is not a precise English equivalent to this type of letter today. The purpose of paranetic letters is the double function of reminding people how they are to behave and of encouraging them in that behavior. Sometimes a paranetic letter will merely repeat general moral advice, and sometimes it will more specifically spell out the behavioral implications of the moral advice that the readers already know is right. For example, as part of Paul's reminder that the Philippians should be living a life in which they experience the peace of God, he urges them to occupy their minds with what is true, honorable, lovely, gracious, and worthy of praise (4:4-8).

Even though most New Testament letters are paranetic, a few are not. The letters of Jude and Second Peter have a very different tone than what we find in those of Paul, James, and John. Jude and Second Peter are more abusive than paranetic. Jude, for example, refers to certain "godless persons" in verse 4, but the author does not actually explain what they do, what they teach, or why his own position is to be preferred. He appeals to his own authority and expects the recipients to accept his judgment without question.

This is in sharp contrast to the style of reasoning we find in Paul, James, or John. In James, for example, we find an exhortation not to judge people by their appearance (Jas 2:1). But James does not end the discussion there by "pulling rank" and moving on to his next instruction. Instead, he gives an illustration of the behavior he objects to and then develops an argument explaining why that behavior is wrong, based on his interpretation of Leviticus 19:18, "You shall love your neighbor as yourself."

In Paul's letters, as well, we can find reasons provided for a desired behavior. Paul's usual procedure is to give reasons and to develop arguments when he is urging some particular action he considers important. Even though he occasionally loses his temper and resorts to name calling (as he does in Phil 3:2, "Beware of the dogs! Beware of the evil-workers!"), Paul still makes an effort to persuade his readers by personal illustrations and by references to what God has accomplished through Christ.

This is not to say that the reasons and arguments given will always be persuasive. For example, Paul's exhortation for women in worship to wear head coverings or veils (1 Cor 11:2-16) seems to be supported by his concern that the angels might lust after women who are not properly covered (v. 10). I find Paul's reasoning difficult either to accept or even to follow. His contention that members of one species (angels) might lust after members of another species (humans) is like saying that a human being might become sexually aroused by looking at a rutabaga. If such a thing were possible on the human-rutabaga level, it would surely be a matter for a human psychotherapist to deal with and not the rutabagas. My own view is that Paul is so convinced that women ought to be wearing head coverings that he introduces as many reasons he can think of to support that position, even when some of the reasons do not make sense. (Paul is not the only biblical author to develop such strange arguments, but this instance is one of the most egregious examples.)

The most common pitfall in interpreting paranetic letters (or paranetic sections within other types of letters) is "mirror reading." Mirror reading involves assuming that any behavior condemned in a letter was actually taking place among the recipients. For example, when the author of 1 Peter 4:15 says, "But let no one among you be made to suffer as a murderer, a thief, an evildoer, or as an intriguer," I do not think we are justified in believing that his readers were murdering, stealing, and practicing sorcery. A paranetic letter usually involves reminding people about what they already know is right. It does not necessarily point to actual problems among a letter's readers. Biblical authors can make it quite clear when they are condemning something that is really taking place (for example, 1 Cor 5:1-13 or Rev 3:14-22).

In interpreting biblical letters, we should always make an initial effort to understand what the letter as a whole is about. By using our imagination, we can ask what the primary effect of the letter was intended to be. Then, in the light of that working hypothesis, we can move on to look at individual sections within the letter. Within paranetic letters we can find personal greetings, chatty narratives, argumentative paragraphs, bursts of temper, occasional teachings, and so on. It may turn out that some of these sections distract from (or even undermine) the author's intention for the letter as a whole; but, nevertheless, they and the overall intent should be considered together.

If we want to focus upon what an author is saying in a specific section within a letter, we must consider the pericope as a whole and ask what its overall purpose was. A series of paragraphs within a letter may be saying, at their most basic level, things like "I thank God for the kindness you have shown me" (as in Phil 1:3-11) or "Don't be misled by people who modify the gospel" (as in Gal 1:6-10).

The important thing to keep in mind, however, is that any given statement within a pericope must be interpreted in terms of how well it fits in with the overall point of the section. To take a single sentence out of context, such as "Wives should be subordinate to their husbands as to the Lord" (Eph 5:22), can cause us to misunderstand an author's overall point. The section of this letter which has this order for wives, in fact, begins with an injunction that husbands and wives are to "be subordinate to one another out of reverence for Christ" (5:21) and contains the exhortation that husbands are to love their wives as Christ loved the church (5:25). The discussion of marriage in Ephesians 5:21-33 does present a hierarchy within marriage, but the author is not as chauvinistic as would appear if one only heard 5:22. Furthermore, if we go on to consider how male dominated the society was in the first century, we may even come to the conclusion that *for his time* the author was unusually sensitive to the idea that marriage involves mutual obligations and responsibilities.

Of the literary categories we have examined so far, the genres of letters and narratives are the most complex. While a proverb or a parable might be as brief as a single sentence, a letter or a narrative could be several thousand words long. And just as a narrative might contain a sermon or a collection of parables, a letter could also have ethical instructions, quotations, or promises. Nevertheless, even in these complex cases of overlapping genres, we must take account of the literary context of any given word or statement we wish to understand. For unless we consider the literary context, there will always be the danger that we shall overlook a message inspired by the Holy Spirit.

CHAPTER 8

Poetry

We normally think of poetry as written material that has rhyme and rhythm. We usually recognize it because it is printed in stanzas with the lines not going all the way to the right-hand margin.

> But poetry is not poetry
> Just because of the way
> It appears on a page.
> There is something more
> To poetry than what meets the eye.

Depending on the edition of the Bible that one reads, one can find dozens of pages of material that are printed in this poetic format. Isaiah, Jeremiah, the Psalms, and Job, among many other books, all have extensive sections of poetry.

But poetic language is not limited to the poems that appear in this easily recognized format. Just because we see words printed from margin to margin without breaks between some of the lines, we cannot assume that what we are reading is not poetry. For example: "Whose woods these are, I think I know. His house is in the village though. He will not see me stopping here, to watch his woods fill up with snow." Even without the clues provided by a particular layout on a printed page, most readers would suspect that those three sentences were not straightforward prose, including those readers who had never heard of Robert Frost.

Poetic language is not exhausted by poems. It has so much energy that it can pop up in almost any type of writing. Poetic language can include not only rhythm and rhyme, but also metaphors, similes, onomatopoeia, alliteration, and many other figures of speech. Appreciating the sound of Hebrew or Greek poetry (in other words, things like its rhyme or rhythm) will be impossible for 99.99 percent of people who read the Bible today. Modern readers bring different skills and education to the study of the Bible, and it is unrealistic to expect all of us to share both expertise in ancient languages and similar aesthetic opinions.

I might as well confess that I have never cared for poetry and so will not comment on the linguistic elegance and beauty of biblical poetry. There are other authors who do. In this chapter I will limit the discussion to making sense of a few figures of speech that can be found in the Bible. I do not deny that there is far more to biblical poetry than what we will examine, but one starts walking by taking individual steps. And beginning a journey by taking individual steps is as necessary for walking across a room as it is for walking across Australia.

The first thing we will probably notice about poetic language in the Bible is its strangeness. The similes we read are not those likely to evoke familiar, or even pleasing, images. (A comparison that uses "like" or "as" is a simile.) For example, consider a few of the similes we can find in the Song of Solomon. The Song of Solomon 4:2 states:

> Your teeth are like a flock of ewes to be shorn,
>   which come up from the washing,
> All of them big with twins,
>   none of them thin and barren.

Such a comparison between teeth and sheep had never occurred to me before I read the Song of Solomon. Even now it sounds odd. But equally strange to our ears probably are Song of Solomon 6:5b and 7:5c.

> Your hair is like a flock of goats
>   streaming down from Gilead.

> Your nose is like the tower on Lebanon
>   that looks toward Damascus.

The strangeness of many of these images comes from the fact that the poetic language of the Bible was written in a very different culture. Many of the rural and agricultural images no longer make any sense. And many of the ancient connotations associated with the words have changed. Comparing someone's hair to a flock of goats a thousand years before Christ was surely meant as a compliment. I am not certain it would be so interpreted today.

The fact of the strangeness in the Bible can be a very useful reminder for those who read it today. In order to understand biblical writers, we must have some sense of their time. Too many Christians simply assume that all parts of the Bible are as equally meaningful in the present as they were in the past. That is not the case. Their world is not our world.

Reading a comparison of someone's nose to a tower in Lebanon reminds us both that towers were once considered beauties of architecture and that Lebanon was once known throughout the world for its glory. When we read other comparisons in the Bible, we should also be aware of the different presuppositions ancient peoples had about war, the roles of men, the roles of women, agriculture, government, and technology.

The most troubling type of poetic language we find in the Bible is the metaphor. A metaphor is a figure of speech where one person, place, or thing is called something else for the purpose of explaining it or highlighting one aspect of its nature. Our greatest problem with metaphors is recognizing them. Similes have a "like" or an "as" to clue us in on the comparison, but we can easily read over metaphors without noticing what is being communicated.

Nonbiblical metaphors in common use are recognized fairly quickly. In *As You Like It* Shakespeare gave us one of the best known: "All the world's a stage, and all the men and women merely players." Shakespeare extended the metaphor to talk about the roles men and women play and how those roles change during the performance. Shakespeare was giving us neither a physical description of the earth ("a stage") nor a metaphysical description of human beings ("merely players"). Instead he was highlighting a particular aspect of human life.

But biblical metaphors are often missed. We frequently make the mistake of thinking that we are reading a scientific (or historical or metaphysical) fact any time the word "is" appears in the Bible. The working hypothesis for many readers of the Bible is that the word "is" means the same thing as the equal sign ("=") in mathematics.

That is a very odd assumption. Consideration of two selections with the word "is" should illustrate its oddness. (I have added italics to the quotations.) "God *is* love" occurs in 1 John 4:16 and is one of the most quoted affirmations of the New Testament. On the other hand, almost never memorized is Leviticus 6:7-8, but it too contains the word we are considering. "This *is* the ritual of the cereal offering. One of Aaron's sons shall first present it before the LORD, in front of the altar. Then he shall take from it a handful of fine flour and oil, together with all the frankincense that is on it, and this he shall burn on the altar as its token offering, a sweet-smelling oblation to the LORD."

I believe that everyone can recognize the fundamental difference between the verb "is" in "God *is* love" and "This *is* the ritual of the cereal offering." The verb in the second quotation preceeds an explanation of the cereal offering. The verb in the first holds the metaphor together. Even though I am convinced of the truth of "God is love" and am willing to debate anyone who denies it, we still must face the fact that God is also called many other things in the Bible: a rock, a warrior, a king, the God of gods, a father, and so on.

If we do not allow for the verb "is" to show us metaphors, we fall into an ocean of logical absurdities. For example, consider what someone who takes "is" as "=" could do with the following two affirmations about God:

1. God = Love.
2. God = A Rock.

Therefore, 3. A Rock = Love.

Evidently, folks in our society are making a major theological error when they send flowers to express affection. The Bible seems to be teaching that we should "say it with rocks." Unless one admits that the simple word "is" often holds a biblical metaphor together, one is going to miss what an inspired author was actually saying. (That is, in addition to making oneself, the Bible, and Christianity itself look ridiculous.)

Knowing that there are metaphors in the Bible, however, does not solve all the problems of understanding what was being said.

Admitting in the abstract that metaphors can be found from Genesis to Revelation does not tell us how to interpret a particular sentence that uses an "is" (or some other form of the verb "to be"). We will still face the problem of deciding which statements are metaphorical and which are not.

Debates are going to continue among Christians about what should be interpreted in a literal sense and what should be interpreted in a metaphorical sense. Among the most troublesome passages will continue to be the following five:

> 1. Jesus' statement during the Last Supper when he held up the bread (Luke 22:19): "This is my body."
> 2. Asaph's statement to the gathered congregation (Ps 82:6): "You are gods, all of you sons of the Most High."
> 3. Jesus' statement during a debate when he was teaching in Jerusalem (John 10:30): "The Father and I are one."
> 4. Jesus' comment to the disciples during the Last Supper when he was telling about the ongoing activity of the Holy Spirit, the Father, and himself (John 14:28): "The Father is greater than I."
> 5. Jesus' public announcement after Peter had declared that Jesus was the Messiah (Matt 16:18): "And so I say to you, you are Peter, and upon this rock I will build my church, and the gates of the netherworld shall not prevail against it."

Differences in interpreting these five sentences have caused deep and even violent disagreements among Christians. We are at the point where many people refuse to allow that anyone can be a Christian unless he or she interprets one (or more) of the above in a literal sense. Yet you can also find people who refuse to admit that anyone can be a Christian unless he or she interprets one (or more) of the above in a metaphorical sense.

This is not the place for me to enter into the theological debates over those statements. My hope is that when people who call themselves Christians find themselves in a heated disagreement about one of the above statements, they stop calling one another names and start talking about *how they know* whether a particular statement was meant in a literal or metaphorical manner. For example, how is it that we know whether the author was expressing himself in a straightforward description of reality or in some sort of poetic language, such as a metaphor? This procedure will not end arguments among Christians, but it will, at the very least, help us to understand one another better.

CHAPTER 9

Prophecy

Although prophecy appears throughout the Bible, and even though prophecy continues to be one of the most regularly mentioned types of literature in the Scriptures, it is probably the most misunderstood biblical genre. Almost everyone thinks that prophecy means predicting the future. The prophets of the Bible are imagined to have been people who had the ability to see into the future. Their major duty, it is commonly believed, was either to predict events in the life of Jesus, usually hundreds of years before he was born, or else to describe events that are to take place in our present time.

This commonly held view of prophecy has an element of truth in it, for much prophecy was meant as a warning from God about the future. Biblical prophets often gave notice to an individual or to a group that unless their behavior changed, they were going to be punished. In addition, the writers of the New Testament regularly explain events from the life of Jesus by pointing out that what occurred took place in order to fulfill prophecy.

But we make a fundamental mistake about the nature of this genre if we think that the prophets' major function was to speak and to write about what was going to take place long after their deaths. The term "prophecy" comes from two Greek words which mean "something brought forth." What the prophets "brought forth" was a message from God. And the message being delivered by a prophet was primarily for those who lived at the same time as the prophet.

To become convinced about the validity of that assertion means that we need to look at the whole work of the particular prophet we are studying. Too often Christians only consider individual verses out of context when they read the prophets and then interpret these verses in relationship to Christ. But when we read an entire prophetic book and ask what its overall effect was intended to be, we can realize how much we may have been missing. To illustrate this approach, let us consider the work of the prophet Amos.

I will concede both that sections of the book of Amos deal with the messianic hopes of its writer and that Christians have traditionally seen Amos 9:11-15 applying to Jesus Christ. Yet the expression of those hopes was not among the major messages of Amos in 750 B.C. While inspired by God, Amos condemned (1) the cruelty of certain business leaders (Amos 2:6b-7a):

> Because they sell the just man for silver,
>   and the poor man for a pair of sandals.
> They trample the heads of the weak
>   into the dust of the earth,
>   and force the lowly out of the way.

(2) the complacency of many of the rich (Amos 4:1):

> Hear this word, women of the mountain of Samaria,
>   you cows of Bashan,
> You who oppress the weak
>   and abuse the needy;
> Who say to your lords,
>   "Bring drink for us!"

(3) the hypocrisy of certain religious leaders, mentioning one of them—Amaziah—by name, (Amos 7:16b-17):

> You say: prophesy not against Israel,
>   preach not against the house of Isaac.
> Now thus says the LORD:
> Your wife shall be made a harlot in the city,
>   and your sons and daughters shall fall by the sword;
> Your land shall be divided by measuring line,
>   and you yourself shall die in an unclean land;
>   Israel shall be exiled far from its land.

(4) the folly of the self-righteous who lived with the comfortable delusion that God was always on their side (Amos 5:21-24):

[The LORD says,] I hate, I spurn your feasts,
  I take no pleasure in your solemnities;
Your cereal offerings I will not accept,
  nor consider your stall-fed peace offerings.
Away with your noisy songs!
  I will not listen to the melodies of your harps.
But if you would offer me holocausts,
  then let justice surge like water,
  and goodness like an unfailing stream.

If we take these specific passages, along with many others also in Amos, there is no trouble in seeing that God was displeased with the people of Israel in the middle of the eighth century B.C. By the words of Amos, God warned the people of Israel, explained how they needed to change, and, among everything else, even offered hope for the future. The book has a complex message. But the fact that God's message then was complex is not an acceptable reason to ignore it today. I believe that societies with complex social and religious problems probably require such complex messages.

If we continue to think about the Book of Amos as a whole, we can also begin to see that Amos' prophecies are based upon what might seem like a rather odd belief about God. The content of Amos' prophecy is based on the presupposition that ethics is not merely a human affair. How human beings treat one another also affects their relationship with God. In fact, one can find material within the prophetic books which suggest that God is the most offended party when people mistreat one another. This presupposition is one that goes against the grain of most modern ethical thought.

Speaking personally, on the basis of a few years of teaching both ethics and biblical studies in college, I have discovered that most students find this idea incredible. Why should God be concerned with human-to-human relations? Many of my students do not see how "it is any of God's business" to be involved in ethics. They, and probably most of the rest of our society, analyze human behavior from the human perspective only and seek answers to contemporary problems from this perspective alone.

But the incredulity with which college students look upon prophecy is less disheartening than the misuse of biblical prophecy, which so often occurs within modern Churches. I do not believe that this misuse is deliberate, but the effect of it is just as damaging to our spiritual lives as if it were. As I see it, there are three primary ways in which prophecy is misunderstood by Christians today.

The first misuse of biblical prophecy involves ignoring its original intent and considering only Christological prophecy as significant. After the resurrection of Jesus, some of the earliest Christians (especially Matthew and Paul) emphasized how many prophecies Jesus had fulfilled. They were attempting to persuade people familiar with the Hebrew scriptures that Jesus had indeed been the Messiah promised by God. They were not trying to interpret the prophets but to evangelize about Jesus.

But too many Christians today misunderstand what Matthew and Paul did and thereby conclude that the New Testament's rather narrow focus on messianic fulfillment is the only method of study appropriate to the prophets. I am not saying that what Matthew or Paul did was wrong. Their focus on certain sections within the prophets was needed for their evangelistic work. It was the task they were called to do. Our modern task, however, is to live out the Christian life in our world. And unless we listen to the total message of the prophets, we are likely to overlook an important part of the gospel.

The second misuse of biblical prophecy does not consist in overlooking what a given passage says but in applying its message to the wrong audience. For example, one could read the passages just quoted from Amos and misinterpret them by saying that they show how bad "the Jews" were and by saying that they let us see the reason why God "rejected the Jews." Even worse than that (but it sometimes is still done), someone could say "the Jews" have always been rich, cruel, and involved with a religious life that displeases God.

Such misinterpretations of the prophets are monstrous. When Christians read the prophets, they need to imagine what abuses of the past gave rise to the prophetic word. And then, when Christians seek to interpret the prophets today, they should make an effort to see what abuses in the present, and especially what abuses in their societies or in their own Churches, might be similar to those of the past. It may be, for example, that some aspects of contemporary American behavior or that certain religious activities of modern Christians are as displeasing to God as anything that occurred in 750 B.C.

The third misuse of biblical prophecy involves considering prophecy as a sort of code that must be broken so that we can figure out when (and how) the world is going to end. While it is true that there is a subcategory within the genre of prophecy that does attempt to reveal how the world will end, there are only a few examples of it within the Bible. This subcategory is the apocalypse. The word "apocalypse" comes from the Greek and means, roughly speaking, a revealed secret. In Daniel, First Thessalonians, Second Thessalonians, and Revelation, we can find apocalyptic sections. It is fair to say that their authors were attempting to tell us a secret about the ultimate fate of the world.

But are we smart enough to figure out what they were saying? I find that I agree with Martin Luther, who once complained that he did not like the final book of the New Testament because "a revelation ought to be revealing" and that Revelation did not live up to its name. Yet the fact that hundreds of attempts to decode Revelation have been published (and proven false) does not stop well-meaning folks from deducing what "666" means or who "the Great Beast" is.

Given that Jesus had the wisdom to say (Mark 13:32), "But of that day or hour, no one knows, neither the angels in heaven, nor the Son, but only the Father," perhaps we would do better to follow his example than that of those people who are claiming (in effect) to know more than he did.

In any case, the genre of the apocalypse is different from most prophecy. But confusing one with the other continues to this day. People who mean well sometimes get so wrapped up in the process of "interpreting" prophecy that they lose track of the gospel. They read all prophecy as if it were apocalyptic literature and become more interested in descriptions about the end of the world than in our responsibilities within the present world.

To some extent this is very understandable. But part of the explanation for being sidetracked from the real message of the prophets is not just a matter of ignorance about genre. We Christians today (and I include myself) do not want to hear the prophets. I do not want to see myself among the cruel, complacent, religious phonies who were condemned by Amos over twenty-eight centuries ago. I do not even want to ask whether the words of Amos might be relevant to my society, my Church, or my life.

Is it any wonder that I would rather use Amos to look into the future? Or that I prefer to use his message to condemn people not of my own nation or religion? Or that I am more comfortable when I can use his words for the sake of giving myself a pat on the back because I had the smarts to see that Jesus fulfilled certain messianic expectations?

Can anyone wonder why we have such a hard time listening to the words of the prophets?

CHAPTER 10

Ethical Instructions

The title of this chapter is deliberately general, and it may seem, to some readers, to be so vague that it is useless. But I wanted a term broad enough to include the more specific literary categories of orders, laws, advice, and commandments. Throughout the Bible one can find hundreds of narratives that contain ethical instructions spoken by a character (or characters) within the stories. Yet one can also find passages in which the author appears to be directly speaking to his readers and telling them how to behave.

At times authors give ethical instructions on their own authority. At other times they claim to be acting on God's authority. A modern reader can find a great deal of ethical instruction that is quite specific, the sort of instruction that is almost like a formula:

In situation S you must do D but not E.

Whenever a person is in situation S, there can be little doubt about how to behave. But Christians today are faced with ethical decisions that can range between what to watch on television tonight and whether to support a particular political candidate. Many of the most specific ethical instructions in the Bible do not seem relevant to our actual circumstances, and many of our specific problems were never considered by any biblical author.

Yet we should not be overly hasty in judging the relevance of ethical instruction in the Bible. It may turn out that the principles of right behavior today might be discoverable among the orders, laws, advice, and commandments given so long ago.

The term "order" in the above list refers to one-time instructions given to a particular person or group. Orders are usually recorded within narratives. Few readers would make the mistake of thinking these orders are relevant today. For example, Luke 19:28-44 tells how Jesus ordered his disciples to bring him a donkey so that he could ride into Jerusalem on Palm Sunday. I have yet to hear of any Christian nowadays who felt compelled to untie donkeys even though Luke 19:30 is unambiguous in its report that this was what Jesus had ordered.

In contrast to the obviously limited applicability of orders, laws were meant to be followed for an extended period of time. Laws also differ from most orders in that they were not given to an individual or a small group but were usually intended for all people within a society. Most of the laws in the Bible are recorded in the Old Testament.

In the Torah (the first five books of the Bible) we can find, among other things, the legal codes of ancient Israel. The people of Israel were supposed to act—both as individuals and as a society collectively—in the manner described by the laws. Examples of these laws would be laws about treating slaves (Exod 21:1-11), making up for a theft (Lev 6:1-7), and protecting natural resources (Exod 23:10-11).

Figuring out what to do now with those laws that were given to ancient Israel is one of the greatest problems in biblical hermeneutics. (Hermeneutics is, put simply, the study of how to apply the Bible today). Should those laws apply or not apply today? Are all, some, or none of them relevant in our contemporary world?

If one does say that some (or all) of the ancient laws apply today, to what situations are they relevant? Should they apply to modern nations, such as Korea and South Africa? Or are they limited to the Christian Church and its members, no matter in what nation they live? Or, since defining who exactly is in the Church would take a lot of effort, do they only apply to individual Christians who feel their consciences leading them to follow the ancient laws?

This is a difficult series of questions. Yet the questions can become even more difficult when one faces the fact that many of the laws have methods of punishment and procedures of establishing guilt (or innocence) that seem strange today. For example, a wife accused of adultery could be tried by being forced to drink a mixture of water, dust, and cereal (Num 5:11-31). She was considered innocent if her abdomen did not swell and she did not have a stomachache. Death was the official penalty for committing adultery. Interestingly enough, the text does not record the procedure for establishing whether a husband was guilty.

My own opinion is that laws given at one time and in one place cannot be taken up wholesale by a different society. Modern societies are built along very different lines than ancient ones. Economic laws prohibiting interest or legal codes describing how a slave owner can punish his slaves no longer make much sense. For better or worse, earning interest on investments seems built into all sectors of our world and national economies, including even Church-sponsored pension plans that count on earning interest to support their retirees. In addition, I have yet to hear Christians argue that slavery should be reintroduced so that we can fulfill the laws about the proper treatment of slaves.

This is not to say that we can ignore the laws we find in the Bible. For many of them could be relevant today. The difficulty is deciding which ones should be followed and which can be ignored. In order to discover which laws are relevant and which ones are not, we need to use some additional standard of moral instruction. By using this supralegal standard we can judge the relevance of the laws recorded in the Bible.

For example, I believe that the laws governing slavery have been nullified, overturned by Jesus' statement of the Golden Rule, "Do unto others as you would have them do unto you." But laws such as those in Leviticus 19:9-16 (about providing food for the poor, theft, honest business practices, respect for the handicapped, and justice within the legal system) seem required by the same statement.

This leads to the next category of ethical instructions: commandments. The most famous examples of this genre are the Ten Commandments. In the commandments we have ethical instruction which seems intended for all people at all times. Commandments are not always specifically named as such in their contexts, but I think it is clear that, say, "Love your neighbor as yourself" was intended as a commandment in both the Old Testament (Lev 19:18) and the New Testament (Matt 22:39, Rom 13:9, Jas 2:8, etc.).

Recognizing the differences among orders, laws, and commandments will take wisdom. There may be times when we do not want to follow some particular ethical instruction and so will be tempted to categorize it as an out-of-date law or as an order that simply does not apply now. The danger of that temptation gives us good reason to study the Bible with groups of Christians and not merely by ourselves. Ethical instructions that seem to have a universal character are likely to be commandments. And when they appear in a variety of contexts and are mentioned by several authors, it becomes more likely that we are dealing with commandments.

But those three genres still leave room for another possible category of ethical instruction: advice. Advice is much harder to deal with. Advice differs from orders in that it has an ongoing character and is not limited to narratives. Advice differs from laws in that it is not meant for a society but for a smaller group, or even an individual, within a larger society. It differs from commandments in that advice usually is tied in with very specific social circumstances.

To illustrate these distinctions we will consider 1 Corinthians 7:1-40, where Paul provides an extended discussion of marriage. In this chapter Paul gives both advice and commandments. He even helps us decide which is which by explaining what he is doing. In verses 6, 8, 12, 17, 25, 32, 35, and 40, Paul either states or implies that he is giving his own advice about the issues at hand. In verses 10, 11, and 15, he either states or implies that he is providing an instruction from God.

But Paul did not follow this pattern throughout his letters. He has left us hundreds of lines of ethical instruction. But which ones did he look upon as his personal advice and which did he consider as being from God? How can we decide between these two possibilities? To put it another way, was Paul more likely to identify his own advice as his own advice or to identify something he looked upon as a commandment from the Lord as being from God? Perhaps he expected that his readers would be able to tell which was which. It is at least possible that he expected his readers to use their common sense, their previous study of the Scriptures, and their personal knowledge of him when they tried to make sense of his letters. (And that probably is just what we now must do ourselves.)

Paul's personal advice is worth listening to. I do not want to imply that his advice may be discarded. But one needs to compare Paul's advice in a given letter with commandments found elsewhere in the Bible or with the advice of some other author that might also apply. Next in the process of understanding Paul's ethical instruction must be an awareness of Paul's historical context. What local situations was Paul faced with? Do the circumstances he faced seem similar to those we face today? It is possible that excellent advice for one time period might be hopelessly inadequate for another.

The same technique illustrated with Paul could be applied when reading other material in the Bible. What did other biblical authors think they were doing when they gave ethical instruction? Did they identify everything they wrote as a permanent instruction from God, meant to be followed by all people at all times? Or did they intend a more limited range of audience and duration?

Even though we have a number of ways to distinguish among the types of ethical instruction, the technique and the questions given above will not meet all the possible difficulties we will face in trying to interpret the Bible. It is at least possible that there were moments in which Paul, for example, thought he was giving a commandment from God but in which he was actually recording his own best judgment at the time. Paul himself is willing to admit that he can get carried away when he becomes overexcited (2 Cor 11:16-12:21). If Paul misunderstood some situation in the ancient Church and thereby made a mistake in his personal advice, surely we would be making an even greater mistake to base our present behavior on what he said in those circumstances.

I regret casting Paul as the heavy in this biblical scenario. He proved his devotion to the cause of Christ in ways that middle-class Americans probably cannot even imagine. The comments and questions I have raised about Paul must also be brought up in reference to the other authors, characters, and events recorded in the Bible. Like it or not, we need to make an effort to interpret the ethical instruction that we find in the Scriptures. Some of it will probably be irrelevant today, but much of it certainly still applies. Our task is figuring out what sort of ethical instruction we are reading.

CHAPTER 11

Theology

Many readers assume that the Bible is full of theology. However, just as many Christians claim "promises" as a result of misunderstanding the genre of some particular passage, it is also true that many other Christians make a mistake when they read a narrative, parable, or whatever, and interpret that passage as if its genre were theology.

Although both types of errors involve mistakes about genre, there is a major difference between these two types of genre misunderstandings. When you claim "promises" that are not actually promises, you usually only hurt yourself. But when you misread dozens of pages from the Bible by taking them as teachings in theology, you have an opportunity to start your own church and to affect far more people.

For almost two thousand years, and especially for the last five hundred years, Christians have argued about the theology of the Bible. Many Churches claim that their theology comes directly from the Bible. One conservative Protestant sect puts it, "We speak where the Bible speaks and are silent where the Bible is silent." The underlying assumption of such statements is that the Old and New Testaments have a theology that can be drawn from a straightforward reading of the Scriptures. Other Christian Churches have said that the Scriptures need to be interpreted by some authoritative body (such as a council of bishops) or by some properly ordained individual in order to make the Bible's theology clear. These

Churches usually find it impossible to speak with one another about theology.

The key to understanding this debate is recognizing that "theology" means different things to different people. Depending on how the term "theology" is defined, many scholars have concluded that there is no theology in the Bible. In the modern and most narrow sense of the term, theology means the same thing as "systematic theology," that is, a scholarly discipline which seeks to provide consistent and convincing explanations about God, humanity, the world, and their mutual interrelationships. In this sense of the word, there is probably no theology in the Bible.

But systematic theology is not what most people have in mind when they talk about theology. We usually use the term to mean statements and opinions about God, humanity, the world, and their mutual interrelationships. The crucial difference between systematic theology and theology is not in the content of their study but in the former's effort to achieve consistency and plausibility.

That difference does not mean that systematic theology is better than theology. After all, the effort to construct a system may be premature if one tries to put things together before all the facts are known. In addition, when one realizes that any theological system must include God, humanity and the world within its area of study, one also needs to face the possibility that the "facts" about these matters may be beyond the human mind's capacity to grasp. And, finally, it may even be the case that the systematic theology of thinkers like St. Augustine or John Calvin is no more profound than the (unsystematic) theology that can be found in the fiction of Fyodor Dostoyevski or C. S. Lewis.

Still, I do not see that the obvious limitations of our knowledge and the probable limitations of our intelligence mean that "anything goes" when it comes to theology. Opinions about God are not like opinions about ice cream. We can all have opinions about what ice cream we like the best, and we can all be right. But some theological opinions are so inconsistent and implausible, or so vicious and narrow-minded, that they deserve to be deconstructed by systematic analysis.

To the best of my knowledge, I have never read any systematic theology in the Bible. No biblical author sought to develop a complete explanation of God, humanity, the world, and their mutual interrelationships. Nonetheless, a modern reader can find a great deal of material in which biblical authors did explore the major questions of life and the universe.

The challenge for Christians today is not finding these passages but making sense of them. For example, Paul never says, "Here is my understanding of God" at the beginning of a few paragraphs where he spells out a coherent and consistent description of the Being who is omniscient, omnipresent, omnipotent, and all-loving. Instead, Paul makes a number of statements about God, Christ, God's relationship to Christ, God's relationship with the Jews and with the Gentiles, God's concern for all humanity, and so on. Making it even more complicated to discover Paul's theology is the fact that these statements can be found in at least a dozen different genres and that they appear in letters that were written over a period of at least twelve years. Those who are interested in Paul's understanding of God must look at all these statements together and attempt to make sense of them.

But the situation with Paul is simpler than that of most other biblical authors. For Paul left us several thousand words in the New Testament. Other writers provided us with only a few hundred. There is simply less to study if one is trying to discover, say, Malachi's understanding of God or Jude's understanding of Christ.

At first one might think that the solution to discovering something quite specific, like Malachi's view of God, is to give up on looking only in Malachi and to broaden one's focus to the whole Bible. One will then say that whatever turns out to be the Bible's understanding of God was a part of Malachi's theology. But what does one do when biblical passages differ from one another?

How, for example, can we make sense of the following four passages that deal with suffering?

(1) Moses is quoted in Deuteronomy 5:9 saying that God punishes sinners and the children of sinners:

> "For I, the LORD, your God, am a jealous God, inflicting punishments for their fathers' wickedness on the children of those who hate me, down to the third and fourth generation."

(2) Ezekiel is quoted in Ezekiel 18:20 speaking the word of the LORD and denying that children are to suffer because of their ancestors' sins:

Only the one who sins shall die. The son shall not be charged with the guilt of his father, nor shall the father be charged with the guilt of his son. The virtuous man's virtue shall be his own, as the wicked man's wickedness will be his own.

(3) Job's suffering is presented as a result of God wanting to prove something to Satan (Job 2:2-6):

And the LORD said to Satan, "Whence do you come?" And Satan answered the LORD and said, "From roaming the earth and patrolling it." And the LORD said to Satan, "Have you noticed my servant Job, and that there is no one on earth like him, faultless and upright, fearing God and avoiding evil? He still holds fast to his innocence although you incited me against him to ruin him without cause." And Satan answered the LORD and said, "Skin for skin! All that a man has will he give for his life. But now put forth your hand and touch his bone and his flesh, and surely he will blaspheme you to your face." And the LORD said to Satan, "He is in your power; only spare his life."

(4) Jesus is quoted in John 9:1-3 answering a question and suggesting that sometimes people suffer so that others may do good for them:

As he passed by he saw a man blind from birth. His disciples asked him, "Rabbi, who sinned, this man or his parents, that he was born blind?" Jesus answered, "Neither he nor his parents sinned; it is so that the works of God might be made visible through him."

These four passages were selected because they illustrate the range of options we can find in the Bible, which we would need to examine before working out a theology of suffering. But how do we make sense of them? We might just pick one and ignore the others. Or we could ignore the Old Testament passages and accept only the New Testament passages. Or we might try to harmonize them all by saying that sometimes Moses is right, and sometimes Ezekiel is right, and so on. But, with this last approach, how would we ever know whether some present suffering was more accurately explained by the view of Moses, Jesus, or Ezekiel?

Understanding biblical theology is not as easy as many Christians think. It is not a matter of shutting your eyes, flopping open the Bible, and putting your index finger on God's message for you today. It is a task that requires looking at different passages and different genres and then going on to try to make sense of them. It also requires study, making an effort to become familiar with the Bible. And by "the Bible" I mean "the whole Bible," not merely those parts that one's tradition favors but also the sections that do not get preached on or were not studied during one's religious education as a child.

Theology is in the Bible. But it is a hidden treasure that must be found before it can be held. Because I am convinced that Jesus is the revelation of God and that the Bible is the record of that revelation, I want to discover what the Bible might have to say about the deepest questions that have concerned human beings. But the Bible does not have a money-back guarantee that anyone can pick it up and find out *all the answers* to *all the questions* he or she might have.

Unfortunately the Bible is not foolproof. Well-meaning folks, and many not-so-well-meaning folks, have used the Bible as the basis for constructing many odd beliefs and practices. They have often used the Bible as a magic mirror that reflected back their own selves and desires. That is an easy way to read the Scriptures, but there is far more to learn when we make the effort to discover what the inspired authors themselves had to say.

CHAPTER 12

Genealogies

Almost everyone who has tried to look up particular passages in the Old Testament has discovered at least one genealogy. Genealogies are the lists of names we usually skip over when we try to read straight through the Scriptures. A genealogy is often called a family tree. But a family tree with unknown names on the branches does not excite anyone, and I will be among the first to admit that the genre of genealogies is probably the least interesting one we can find in the Bible.

Knowing that the sons of Gomer were Ashkenaz, Riphath, and Togarmah (Gen 10:3) probably matters to someone, but I have not met that person yet. At the same time, genealogies are very easy to recognize and, more importantly for our purposes here, knowing something about the literary character of genealogies can serve as a warning about what happens when you try to take the Bible "literally."

In order to understand this genre, we must make a distinction between biblical genealogies and modern genealogies. A modern family tree is intended to be an accurate record of one's biological ancestors. It is crucial for these modern records to show one's grandmothers and great-grandfathers and great-great-whatevers in their proper order. These records must contain information that is as biologically precise as possible.

Knowing the biological ancestry of someone can be very useful for physicians and scientists who are attempting to trace a genetically transmitted problem or condition. On the basis of modern genealogical research, it has been found that Huntington's chorea, for example, is an inherited disorder but that Lou Gehrig's disease (which is also known as ALS or amyotrophic lateral sclerosis) cannot be proved to have been transmitted genetically.

Family trees in the Bible do not serve the same function as these scientific genealogies. Both types of genealogies (that is, the modern ones and biblical ones) give us valuable information, but the information is not at all the same. In fact, we would have a better idea of how to read biblical genealogies if we thought about them listing ancestors in a spiritual or symbolic sense rather than in a biological sense.

There are modern parallels to this notion of spiritual or symbolic ancestors. Consider the two great national holidays of the United States: the Fourth of July and Thanksgiving. Now, as far as my family has been able to learn, my biological ancestors came over in the middle of the nineteenth century hoping to escape poverty in Britain. Yet on the Fourth of July I am very willing to think of and speak of "our ancestors" who declared their independence in 1776. And on Thanksgiving I can also consider the Pilgrims and the Native Americans as "our ancestors." On that day I can join in the common hope that the dream of sharing with one another and thanking God for our blessings could unite all Americans in the present time.

If someone were to corner me and object to my speaking of "our ancestors" in reference to Thanksgiving or the Fourth of July because the McGehee family were latecomers, I would say that by "ancestors" I meant those men and women who were my spiritual ancestors and not my biological ancestors. Even if I kept my temper and said nothing further, I would surely think that the kind of person who would make such a pedantic objection about biological ancestry was someone who did not have much feeling for the spiritual side of things.

The best evidence that the biblical writers thought of genealogies in this symbolic sense can be seen in the fact that the names and sequences in genealogies sometimes differ even within the Bible. For example, in Joshua 14:6 and Numbers 14:31 a certain Caleb is mentioned and described as a son of Jephunneh. Caleb was not an Israelite but a Canaanite who helped the Israelites settle in the Promised Land. But in the later work of First Chronicles, Caleb's "ancestry" has changed. He is listed as an Israelite and the son of Hezron (2:18 and 2:42). Caleb's heroic activities led to him being considered *symbolically* an Israelite and his genealogy in later material was changed to reflect that.

The fact that Caleb's family tree is presented in two quite different ways will bother almost no one who reads the Bible. But there are two genealogies in the New Testament that can lead to fierce arguments, especially when their differences are pointed out. The genealogies are those of Jesus.

The first genealogy appears in Matthew 1 and the second is in Luke 3. If we compare the names in the two lists, it will not take long to discover that the names differ. The most obvious discrepencies are that the names of Joseph's father are not the same and that the lineage from King David is traced through different sons of David. Matthew traces Jesus' ancestry through the royal family, Luke does not.

Matthew's Version	*Luke's Version*
David the King	David the King
Solomon	Nathan
Rehoboam	Mattatha
Abijah	Menna
•	•
•	•
•	•
Jacob	Heli
Joseph	Joseph

If we do a little more research and compare these two New Testament genealogies with the genealogies of some of the most important characters in the Old Testament, other differences also appear. For example, the list of ancestors from Perez to King David in Luke 3:32-33 is not the same as in Ruth 4:18-22. Matthew 1:3-6, on the other hand, does agree with the genealogy in Ruth.

But does that really prove that Matthew's genealogy is more accurate than Luke's? The question is intriguing, but we cannot answer it by comparing only the genealogies in Matthew and Ruth. For Matthew's list of kings from David to Jechoniah does not include a number of the kings whose history can be found in First and Second Kings and First and Second Chronicles. In addition, there is a certain pattern to his list. Matthew typically leaves out the names of the worst kings.

If we read these genealogies of Jesus according to our modern standards of family trees and expect to find exact biological relationships, we probably have to conclude that these lists are in obvious contradiction. But if we read the genealogies of Jesus as the literary attempts of Luke and Matthew to describe Jesus' symbolic heritage, we do not run into the theological problem of wondering whether or not we must reject one of the traditional genealogies. It seems clear (to me, at least) that Matthew intended to show that Jesus was of the royal family, had a legitimate claim to the throne, and thereby fulfilled one of the expectations associated with the Messiah. In contrast, Luke wanted to show that Jesus' symbolic heritage was through the spiritual leaders of Judah and that he had fulfilled the messianic expectations associated with the non-ruling families who remained true to God.

In the spiritual sense that the evangelists intended for us to read the genealogies in their Gospels, there is no contradiction. For it not only is possible but also is *in fact* true that Jesus was symbolically descended from both the royal line and the "family" of spiritual leaders in Judah.

Even though these comments about the genre of genealogies can free us from certain theological difficulties, it is still true that different understandings of genealogies have caused problems within the Christian Churches. For over sixteen hundred years there have been Christians who argued that Luke was giving Mary's biological genealogy and Matthew giving Joseph's biological heritage. Such a contention is often made today by people who claim to take the Bible literally.

There are two different replies to make to this contention. The best reply is to say that this theory cannot be supported by what we find in the Bible. First of all, Luke and Matthew neither indicate nor even imply that they want to say anything about the biological relationship of Jesus with his ancestors. In fact, both of them contain narratives in which Jesus' birth is described as a miracle in which a virgin gave birth. Joseph's relationship to Jesus, according to Luke and Matthew, is not a biological one. Therefore, whether Joseph's father was Heli or Jacob is not that important *in a scientific sense* since neither could have been the biological grand-father of Jesus.

Secondly, I find it strange that some of the Christians who are so concerned about protecting the "literal truth" of the Bible have to do so by arguing that when Luke wrote "Joseph" he meant "Mary." A theory of inspiration that claims to be literalistic and yet assumes that "Joseph" = "Mary" *every now and then* is a theory which does not need to be argued against. I think such a theory literally contradicts itself.

We are much more likely to discover the meaning of what Luke and Matthew were saying if we recognize that they were following the standard way of writing genealogies in the Bible. Biology was not their interest. They were showing us a more important type of relationship when they gave us Jesus' spiritual heritage.

CHAPTER 13

Quotations

Before we begin exploring how quotations in the Bible can be interpreted, we need to become more specific about the meaning of the term. There are two primary meanings for "quotations." The first refers to the words that appear in a dialogue spoken by characters in some narrative. In the longer biblical narratives, such as Mark or First Samuel, we can find a number of statements, questions and answers, speeches, prayers, and so on, all of which have quotation marks indicating where they begin and end. The second kind of "quotations" involves the repetition of material originally written or spoken by someone earlier. Most of the quotations we will consider in this category were made by New Testament authors who incorporated selections from the Old Testament into their own letters, narratives, prophecies, or ethical instructions.

It is not difficult to interpret the first kind of quotations (that is, when characters are quoted speaking in a dialogue). These quotations are meant to give the reader a sense of what was being said. They need to be interpreted within the context of the pericope in which they appear and should not be read as isolated promises, ethical instructions, or whatever. Many statements within quotation marks simply do not tell the truth. For example, a character may be quoted when telling a lie (as Satan is in Gen 3) or may be quoted when giving the wrong interpretation to some event (as Job's friends do throughout the Book of Job). Therefore, a reader must not focus on the individual quotations attributed to a specific character within a passage but look at the message of the narrative as a whole.

When one looks at each narrative as a whole, one does not need to get bogged down in pointless discussions about the exact words that were said at a given place and time. The overall meaning of a passage is what is important. For example, consider the narrative about Jesus' calming of a storm at sea. This narrative appears in Matthew 8:23-27, Mark 4:35-41, and Luke 8:22-25.

Although the plot is basically the same in all three accounts, the individual words within quotation marks differ among the Gospels. In Matthew the disciples seek help from Jesus by waking him and saying, "Lord, save us! We are perishing!" In Mark they ask a question, "Teacher, do you not care that we are perishing?" And in Luke the disciples ask for help saying, "Master, master, we are perishing!" In all three accounts Jesus is addressed by means of a title and the word "perishing" is used; but the exact wording of the disciple's plea for help differs, as does the title used in reference to Jesus—Lord, Teacher, or Master. A modern reader can find literally hundreds of differences like this in the wording of quotations throughout the Gospels.

But biblical writers never claimed that their dialogues were meant to be exact word-for-word quotations of what actually was said during some event. I believe that they did not make such a claim because they assumed that no one would expect them to be recording exactly the words that had been used. There were no people walking around with tape recorders or video cameras back then. When the writers of the Gospels did their research into the events of Jesus' life, they probably were faced with spoken accounts and written records that differed. These sorts of differences are similiar to those faced today by courts of law, reporters, and parents who must try to figure out what happened during some event on the basis of testimony that does not always agree.

Because of the obvious differences within gospel dialogues, if Matthew, Mark, Luke, and John had claimed to be recording the exact words of Jesus' life, we would have to conclude that *at least* three of them failed to tell the truth. But, since they never make such a claim, we can read their Gospels with the conviction that they are giving us a reliable interpretation of the life of Jesus. We discover the truth about Jesus not by focusing on whether he was called "Lord," "Teacher," or "Master," but instead by looking at the meaning of the gospel narratives as a whole.

The second type of biblical quotations do not necessarily have their boundaries set off by quotation marks, but recognizing them is usually not difficult. These are repetitions of material that originated elsewhere. Many Bibles have footnotes that indicate where a given statement originally appeared. But looking back at the original context does not explain why a later author quoted from the earlier source. In fact, if we want to understand a quotation, we must first have some idea about what the quotation was supposed to do *in the later work*.

This effort requires us to keep in mind that a quotation has both an original and a later context, and also that a quotation must be interpreted differently if the genre of these two contexts varies. This is as true for interpreting quotations today as it is for interpreting New Testament quotations. It should be easy to see that a statement and the later quotation of that statement might have differing meanings if we consider some examples.

Since quotations are a type of literature common in both the modern and ancient worlds, we can begin thinking about the literary functions of quotations by considering why people use them today. Well, as Virgil expressed it so well, "*Non omnia possumus omnes.*"

Now, whether or not that Latin quotation irritated you enough to hurl this book against the wall, you probably grasped the point that people can quote things in order to show off. College professors, newspaper columnists, and certain kinds of writers do it all the time. I doubt, however, that any New Testament authors quoted material for that reason.

Quotations are also used when people argue, or, to put it less dramatically, when they are trying to prove something. Quotations are heard frequently when people debate anything from politics to religion. Some of these quotations are so powerful that they can end a debate. It takes a rare person in a college classroom to disagree with any statement that follows "Well, as Einstein said . . ." And not many Christians in a theological discussion ever dismiss a sentence that follows "Yes, but Jesus said . . ." Yet quotations need not end a discussion; they can also support the case an individual is making. In these circumstances quotations function as evidence or as appeals to authority.

Such uses appear most frequently in the New Testament. In James 2:8 the author quotes Leviticus 19:18, "You shall love your neighbor as yourself," to clinch his argument that Christians should not discriminate against the poor. And in Mark 10:7-8, during a discussion about divorce, Jesus quotes Genesis 2:24, "For this reason a man shall leave his father and mother [and be joined to his wife], and the two shall become one flesh." The original context in Genesis dealt with marriage, but Jesus has put the stress of the quotation on the last clause ("the two shall become one flesh") and has made it a major part of his explanation about divorce.

The most common usage of Old Testament quotations in the New Testament follows the same pattern of presenting evidence in order to make a point. Throughout the Gospels, especially, one can find statements like Matthew 1:22, "All this took place to fulfill what the Lord had said through the prophet . . ." That sort of introduction is then followed by a quotation from the Old Testament. These quotations were intended to function as evidence that Jesus was the promised Messiah.

But quotations can also be brought up with the intent of refuting the quotation. In order to explain my own faith to an agnostic, I might quote Friedrich Nietzsche's provocative question, "Is man only a blunder of God, or God only a blunder of man?" The purpose of quoting Nietzsche would be to make his philosophy explicit so that I could explain why I disagree.

Paul did the same thing in 1 Corinthians 15:33 when he quoted a well-known slogan associated with Epicurean philosophers: "Let us eat and drink, for tomorrow we die." No one who reads the chapter where that statement appears would ever think that Paul was endorsing that lifestyle. Jesus, I think, was doing something similar in Matthew 5:38 when he quoted Exodus 21:24, "An eye for an eye and a tooth for a tooth." Jesus followed this by saying: "But I say to you, offer no resistance to one who is evil. When someone strikes you on [your] right cheek, turn the other one to him as well."

Still other functions of quotations can be found. Sometimes we quote something because we wish to modify it, bring it up to date, or expand on its meaning. The Supreme Court does this regularly when it quotes from the First Amendment, "Congress shall make no law respecting an establishment of religion, or prohibiting the free exercise thereof," and then states how those phrases apply today.

Jesus did this sort of thing in Matthew 5:27 when he quoted Exodus 20:14, "You shall not commit adultery." Jesus modified the statement's original intent, which was to condemn the particular action of adultery, by expanding its jurisdiction to include willfully lusting after another person. In Acts 17:28 Paul is presented doing something similar as well, but in this case Paul is not quoting from the Old Testament. Instead, he is quoting two non-Christian Greek writers, Epimenides and Aratus.

Both Paul and Jesus used these quotations as the starting point for further remarks. However, not only did their quotation of earlier material serve as the logical basis for further ideas, but it also gave them a chance to connect with the people who were listening. By quoting material that was familiar to and honored by their audiences, they established the common ground to begin a dialogue. If Paul or Jesus had just started off by giving their own ideas without the quotations, especially to hostile or indifferent audiences, they would have been far less persuasive speakers.

Yet there is still another kind of reason behind people's use of quotations. The remark from Virgil, which I quoted above, "We are not all capable of everything," can help us clarify a somewhat different reason for using quotations. Some writers have such an ability to express complex ideas in short, clear sentences that less concise writers (those of us who are used to rambling on from one vague idea to another) like to use quotations as a means of improving our prose. An apt quotation can convey as much information as a computer chip.

Quotations used in this way can summarize what has been said, can foreshadow what will be said, or can illustrate what is being said. One of the best examples of a quotation being used to illustrate a point can be found in Philippians 2:6-11. This early Christian hymn (recognized because of its non-Pauline vocabulary and its peculiar rhythmic pattern) is quoted by Paul in order to illustrate the proper behavior Christians should exhibit toward one another. After mentioning the name of Christ Jesus, Paul states:

> Who, though he was in the form of God,
>   did not regard equality with God something to be grasped.

Rather, he emptied himself,
taking the form of a slave,
coming in human likeness;
and found human in appearance,
he humbled himself,
becoming obedient to death,
    even death on a cross.
Because of this, God greatly exalted him
and bestowed on him the name
that is above every name,
that at the name of Jesus
every knee should bend,
of those in heaven and on earth and under the earth,
and every tongue confess that,
Jesus Christ is Lord,
to the glory of God the Father.

In interpreting this passage, the first question to ask is the same one we ask when we discover any other quotation: "Why is this material here?" Unless our answer to that question is based on the realization that Paul has quoted this hymn in order to illustrate Jesus' humility and obedience as an example for us, we may develop some very odd ideas about Jesus.

This passage was not meant to teach us about the metaphysical nature of Jesus. It was never meant as systematic theology. It was used to give us an example to follow. If we make the mistake of seeing this as a theological statement about Jesus, we would have to conclude that Jesus had not been a real human being. The hymn says that he had come "in human likeness," but there is a big difference between being in human likeness and being human. A statue, a portrait, or a robot could all be made to look human, but that would not make them human.

Paul quoted the hymn not because he agreed with all the presuppositions it implied but because he wanted to make his own point about humility. If we constructed a Christology based on taking the hymn in Philippians 2 as Paul's major teaching about the metaphysical nature of Jesus, we would probably come up with the first great heresy faced by Christianity: Docetism. (Docetism comes the Greek word *dokeo* which means "I seem" or "I appear.") This kind of theology said that Jesus had not been a real man but had only seemed to be a human being. Such a theology not only does not agree with what Paul says elsewhere but also goes against the manner in which Jesus was presented in the Gospels. The main problem with Docetism is that if Jesus was not truly human, his suffering and death lose much of their meaning. He would not have been able to identify with us if he had been something which only seemed human.

To sum up, when a quotation appears in the New Testament, it may be there because the author agrees with it, disagrees with it, or both partly agrees and partly disagrees with it. There is no way to tell what the author's position is unless we read the quotation in its complete, later context. Was the author using the quotation to prove a point? Was he attempting to refute it? Was he using it as a basis on which to develop some related idea? Or did he agree with one particular aspect of the quotation but not with all the other ideas implied? Only after we answer the question of why an author used a quotation can we move on to ask what the author intended to say.

CHAPTER 14

Sermons

In contrast to hymns, which are often the favorite part of worship services for many Christians, sermons are seldom what we look forward to when we attend church. There are a number of reasons for preferring hymns to sermons. Sermons sometimes challenge people to make unwanted changes in their lives. And while hymns usually affirm us and make us feel involved in the Christian life, sermons can remind us that we are not living up to our calling. In addition, there are many other reasons why people prefer hymns to sermons. Sermons can be poorly delivered, inadequately prepared, or just plain dumb.

Yet sermons have been around for a very long time and seem to be the best way of communicating certain specific kinds of messages. But before we examine some sermons from the Bible and make an effort to intrepret them, I think that it would be worthwhile to consider what sort of things contemporary sermons communicate and how well they do what they are supposed to do. Since the sermon is one of the few biblical genres that can be found today, we can understand ancient sermons better if we first think about modern sermons.

When I was in the seminary, the basic lesson of the course in preaching was that a sermon is not a lecture. A lecture is designed to teach something. While a sermon can attempt to teach something new, a sermon could also be doing many other things. A sermon can comfort people in suffering, or encourage them to continue doing what is right, or remind them of something they already knew was right but have not been doing. The general word for those three activities (comforting, encouraging, and reminding) is exhortation. In a sermon a minister should be exhorting the congregation.

In order to succeed in its exhortation, the sermon must provide reasons for the desired result. If a pastor wants people to be comforted in hard times, examples of others in suffering and how they overcome adversity could be used. The sermon could contain stories from the Bible, say, about Job or Hannah. The congregation might be reminded of biblical promises about a life to come or about finding God's peace now.

If, however, a pastor wants people to make a change in behavior, there are other ways of convincing them about the need for change. The sermon may show how some common behavior, the sort of thing that "everyone does," is actually causing harm. A pastor might appeal to a congregation's better instincts and point out that loving others requires that we make changes in our lives. Or one could give up the idea of working on our better instincts altogether and instead point out the possible consequences of following the crowd or of doing nothing. Bad things can happen to good people. And there are times when our behavior brings harm on ourselves. A preacher may sometimes have the responsibility to make us aware of that.

The fact that a sermon should not be a lecture means that its primary purpose is something other than giving information. Information may be communicated in a sermon, but good sermons usually do more than that. No matter what sort of exhortation is involved, in order for the sermon to succeed, there must be an element of persuasion in it. Whether a speaker is comforting, encouraging, or reminding a congregation, he or she needs to persuade them about something. Perhaps the members of a community need to see that current suffering will pass, or that they can accomplish what seems difficult, or that they should remember what they have conveniently forgotten.

But there needs to be a balance between having the sermon persuade the congregation and respecting the feelings and intellects of the congregation. Some techniques of persuasion are unfair. The very effective means of persuading people that we see on television, say, to buy new cars or designer clothes, and which often involve snob appeal or sexual exploitation, are out of place. But legitimate persuasion can be done by many different rhetorical devices: quoting a Scripture, referring to an expert, repeating key ideas, rephrasing key ideas, developing logical arguments, exaggerating major points, giving a list of reasons, focusing on one side of an issue, using humorous stories, and so on.

There are a number of sermons in the Bible. Among the most famous are Jesus' Sermon on the Mount in Matthew 5–7, Jesus' Sermon on the Plain in Luke 6:20-49, the sermon recorded in Nehemiah 9:5–10:39, and the book of Deuteronomy. The books of the prophets are also full of sermons. In addition, although the New Testament Book of Hebrews is often called "The Letter to the Hebrews," it is actually the copy of a sermon with a P. S. written on the end at 13:22-25. (To see that the genre of Hebrews is not a letter, contrast its beginning with those of Paul's letters or the brief letters in Revelation 2–3, and then compare how similar Hebrews 13:20-21 is to the benediction in a modern sermon.)

The key to interpreting sermons, whether in the Bible or not, is to discover what the sermon was intended to accomplish. After hearing or reading a sermon, it is always a good idea to ask, "What am I now supposed to feel, do, or think?" An effective sermon will have delivered a clear message, and answering the question about its intended effect should not take a lot of time.

The major problem that prevents us from understanding a sermon, though, is only paying attention to parts of it. Since a sermon is supposed to be a unified whole that gets a message across, if we merely look at parts of the whole, we may misunderstand the message. And since sermons often use rhetorical devices in order to strengthen the force of their exhortation, if we put undue emphasis on an exaggeration or a quotation or a humorous story in a sermon, we will probably miss the point.

For example, even biblical sermons often contain exaggerations. We might as well start with an example that will irritate some readers, but I think it can illustrate the situation perfectly. Consider Jesus' remarks about lust in the Sermon on the Mount (Matt 5:28-30):

> "But I say to you, everyone who looks at a woman with lust has already committed adultery with her in his heart. If your right eye causes you to sin, tear it out and throw it away. It is better for you

to lose one of your members than to have your whole body thrown into Gehenna. And if your right hand causes you to sin, cut it off and throw it away. It is better for you to lose one of your members than to have your whole body go into Gehenna."

If we act on the assumption that Jesus really made these comments about lust, why is it that we so seldom come across Christians who are without eyes or hands? Surely there are only a few people who would argue that it is because lust is never a problem for Christians. Why, then, do we disobey Jesus?

The answer is that Christians recognize that Jesus was not speaking literally. Not for a moment do I believe that Jesus intended for us to pluck out our eyes or cut off our hands to avoid lust. This is, in fact, one of the few passages that almost all Christians have recognized as needing a nonliteral interpretation. That kind of interpretation is the only one that makes sense. For one thing, Jesus certainly knew that hands and eyes are not the organs that cause the most trouble in this matter. But, even more importantly, Jesus used this exaggeration deliberately in order to make his listeners realize how serious a thing sin was. He expected them to react with horror when they imagined what it would be like to cut off a hand, but he also wanted them to move beyond that emotional reaction and go on to make a comparison between the relative value of one's hand and the value of one's soul.

Yet, even though almost all modern readers, just by using their common sense, know that Jesus was exaggerating in this passage, many of us cannot admit out loud that other exaggerations may also exist. This unwillingness to read the Bible on its own terms leads to a lot of the exaggerations (and other rhetorical devices) in biblical sermons being misunderstood.

For example, Hebrews 6:4-8 and 10:26-31 are passages in which the author indicates that Christians will not be able to receive forgiveness for sins deliberately committed after being saved. These frightening words have caused many sleepless nights for believers. But once one realizes that these passages are sections within a sermon and are, in fact, exaggerations, which were used in order to stress the seriousness of sin, one sees that they were not meant to be taken literally.

Additional evidence that this material from Hebrews is exaggerated can be seen by comparing it with other biblical texts.

Throughout the New Testament, but especially in the ethical instruction of Paul or in passages like 1 John 2:1, writers have made it clear that Christians can (and should) repent of their sins. And Jesus himself is quoted, in sermons and in prayers and in other genres, urging us to forgive others so that we, too, might experience God's forgiveness. If the forgiveness of sins were not possible (or our committing of sins impossible!), it would have been senseless for Jesus to talk so much about them.

Although there are a number of rhetorical devices that can be found in biblical sermons, we should not assume that everything is exaggerated. I believe that Jesus told the absolute truth, but by means of a metaphor, when he said (Matt 6:24), "No one can serve two masters. He will either hate one and love the other, or be devoted to one and despise the other. You cannot serve God and mammon." Jesus is telling us that we will have to make a choice between seeking financial success and seeking God when we decide on the ultimate purpose of our lives.

I wish there were a complete description of all the exaggerations and other rhetorical devices that can be found in the Bible's sermons. It would be very nice to know if Jesus was exaggerating when he spoke about turning the other cheek (Matt 5:39) or about the wrongness of divorce (Matt 5:31-32).

Unfortunately, since we do not know what kind of inflection or gestures Jesus used when he made these comments, I do not see that we will ever be able to have absolute certainty in our interpretation. But by considering what the Gospels tell us about Jesus elsewhere and by considering what other biblical writers have to say, we can come very close to understanding the message we were supposed to hear. This same method of comparing and contrasting the content of a sermon to other Scriptures is our best way of interpreting any biblical sermon.

CHAPTER 15

History

The Bible is full of history. But there is less history than some people think, and more history than others might believe. This paradox is an accurate statement of the situation because, in part, even the term "history" is ambiguous. On the one hand, history is everything that has happened. In this sense, because the Bible itself is a book from the past, the entire Bible is history. On the other hand, and more importantly, history is a record of the past that attempts to provide a reasonable interpretation of people, events, and ideas. In this sense, history is a genre that can be found (along with many other types of literature) in the Bible. It is history in this sense of the word that will be examined here.

History is a particular type of narrative. As a category within the overarching genre of narrative, history is distinctive because it is based in fact, while a narrative can be either fiction, nonfiction, or something with elements of both. In the Bible the most common fictional narratives are the parables, and the most common nonfiction narratives are history. Two types of biblical narratives that have elements of both fiction and nonfiction are the legends and the myths. We shall examine the genre of myths and how to interpret them in the next chapter. But because legends are so similar to history, we will compare the two of them later in this chapter.

In spite of what many people believe before they actually begin to think about it, history is not a complete collection of facts about the past. No history could ever tell the whole story of even a minor human event, say, a family eating dinner at a fast-food restaurant.

There would not be room on a million pages to describe *fully* the second-by-second changes in the thoughts and feelings, the biochemistry of those thoughts and feelings, the chemistry of digestion, the length of every strand of hair, the texture and color of the clothing, the previous educational experiences, and the sociological characteristics of each of the human beings eating their dinner. Then, when you remember to include explanations detailing how and from where the plastic, paper, hamburger, buns, grain, wheat, lettuce, potatoes, and deep-fat fryers came to be in that particular restaurant, you realize that to describe this dinner completely you must also give reports on the development of the earth's plant and animal life, the advance of human technology, and a description of contemporary business practices.

Those who have attempted to write history have long recognized that the overwhelming mass of data associated with any human event cannot be fully recorded. One of the most profound New Testament authors admitted this limitation in John 21:25: "There are also many other things that Jesus did, but if these were to be described individually, I do not think the whole world would contain the books that would be written." Because a historian cannot totally describe any event, the historian must select what he or she considers to be the most important things going on at a given time. But what the historian considers most important depends on what kind of history is being written. Describing a dinner at a fast-food restaurant will be very different if one is writing a report on the American family in general, a history of deep-fat fryers in particular, or a biography about a member of the (hypothetical) family who grew up to become the first woman president and who remembered that particular meal because she first announced her plan to become president while eating french fries.

A historian not only selects what part of the complete facts to tell but also attempts to explain why and how that selection was made. In addition, well-written history seeks to put things in some kind of context. It does this by asking what led up to the event, what contemporary factors influenced it, and what its significance was.

Knowing these things about history helps us to see that any history is going to provide only a partial explanation of an event, person, or idea. Some explanations may be narrower and less persuasive than others. Historians usually differ about what is the most important thing to say about an event and about how to interpret the event. The practical consequence for readers then is that we need to be alert to what a writer intended to do in a given historical passage and what sort of explanation he or she was presenting.

Consider the historical account in Exodus 14 of Israel's flight from Egypt under Moses. I accept it as true that the people who were looked upon as Israel's ancestors left Egypt against the will of Egyptian leaders. And I accept the claim that part of the escape involved the Israelites crossing the Red Sea in a way that was denied the Egyptian soldiers. The explanation given in the text is that this was done by God.

Except for saying that there had been a mighty wind, however, the text does not tell us exactly how God accomplished this event. For example, did God create this wind out of nothing or did it result from normal meteorological phenomena that God arranged to occur *at this particular time?* The text does not give us a complete explanation. Further, if Egyptian historians recorded the escape, I suspect that they would have interpreted it very differently. They might have focused on the difficulty of moving chariots through mud, or said that the Hebrews were not worth going after, or spoken of how their god Osirus was punishing the Pharaoh for some impiety.

The Exodus can be interpreted in many different ways. History needs to be true to what happened, but the real room for disagreement comes when historians attempt to explain why something happened. Biblical history, which regularly makes claims that God had been involved in some particular event, was written by believers who interpreted events a certain way. Even when other historians agree on what happened, when it happened, and who was involved, they will probably disagree on why it happened. In that sense, accepting any biblical history as true requires a faith commitment. Readers who are skeptical can always doubt any historical explanation that brings God into the account.

In addition, when historians are writing, they never have complete information. This occurs not only with quotations but also with chronology and even, sometimes, with the events themselves. The ancient Greek writer Thucydides, who is usually called the Father of History, stated the rule that has become standard for historians dealing with incomplete or contradictory information. Historians are expected to use their best judgment in selecting which information and interpretations they consider most probable. Furthermore, if the exact words that were spoken during an event were lost, one was allowed to paraphrase speeches or dialogues that made the most sense, given the circumstances of the event.

Knowing that writing history means both making a selection from an incomplete set of the facts and developing an interpretation based on the historian's best judgment can help us interpret history in the Bible. A detailed comparison of Ezra with Nehemiah or of First and Second Kings with First and Second Chronicles shows a number of differences in names, events, and chronology. But differences among histories also occur in the New Testament. The Gospels of Matthew, Mark, Luke, and John all tell the story of Jesus. But they differ in terms of exact quotations from Jesus, chronology, locations, and even incidents.

If we approach the Gospels with a preset definition of history, one that does not conform to what historians actually do, we will have to conclude that the Gospels are not history. But if we see that history involves the selection of information, different interpretations of events, and the possibility of creating dialogue, we can see that the Gospels are indeed history. Each of the authors was making choices about what to tell and what to leave unsaid. And at times each used his best judgment to tell what happened and what exact words were said.

For example, the narrative of Jesus' entry into Jerusalem before his crucifixion can be found in all four Gospels. But Mark 11:1-10 and Luke 19:28-38 quote Jesus differently in his instructions to bring a donkey for him to ride on. Then, while Matthew 21:1-9 has Jesus asking his disciples to bring two animals, a donkey and her foal, John 12:12-19 reports that Jesus himself "found" the donkey he rode on.

Recognizing that differences like these (and there are hundreds of them) can be found throughout the Bible does not undermine my faith. That is because the genre of history involves human beings making judgments about what gets recorded and how it is reported. I am convinced that God has been involved in past events, like the Exodus from Egypt or the resurrection of Jesus. But because biblical history is similar to other types of history, I expect that history in the Bible will have some differences in interpretation and even in the facts reported. After all, the gospel writers were never attempting to get all the details right in their stories about fetching donkeys. They had other, more important concerns.

Their interest was in convincing us that Jesus was the Christ, who would be the Savior of the world. That point is made explicitly in John 20:30-31. "Now Jesus did many other signs in the presence of [his] disciples that are not written in this book. But these are written that you may believe that Jesus is the Messiah, the Son of God, and that through this belief you may have life in his name."

It may be that some Christians reading this chapter will object to the explanation of history I have outlined above. They could say that "history" is a different genre depending on whether it is written by human beings or written by God. I will admit that possibility.

However, if someone wants to say something like "Man's histories can vary but God's history is perfect," that person is faced with two major problems. The first is inventing another term for this genre of "God's history," since it is going to be different from any other type of history. The work of historians involves researching, thinking, evaluating, judging, and writing. Since God would not need to do any of the first four activities, it seems to me that "history" would be a misleading term to use in reference to any work of which God was the sole author.

The second but far more serious problem is how we make sense of the differences that occur throughout the historical sections of the Bible. This is not just a matter of fetching donkeys; it also involves hundreds of variations in quotations, names, dates, and places. If we start with the assumption that God is directly responsible for every word in these sections, we are going to wind up with some very strange ideas about God. However, if we start with the assumptions that God has been involved in human life and that writers (as human beings) have done their best to make sense of that involvement, the variations in the Bible no longer undermine convictions about God's wisdom, power, or love.

Misinterpreting history in the Bible can tend to weaken those convictions. For example, the primary danger in interpreting biblical history is assuming that what people did, or what God said (or what people claimed God said), is to be followed today. You can pour over Old Testament accounts of ancient warfare until you start to feel queasy, but surely it is going too far to assume that because ancient war was conducted along certain lines, we are commanded to practice war in the same way. I have yet to hear a minister (or military chaplain) argue that Christians in the army should follow the ancient Israelite practice of killing all men, women, and children in certain captured towns.

Why, then, were some of the horrible events of biblical history recorded? My own view is that some of these accounts were recorded, under God's inspiration, to serve as bad examples for us. That is, they show what people were willing to claim God was saying. Very often "God" was saying the very thing that would give some sort of financial or political benefit to those who spoke for God. At times these beliefs were probably quite sincere. But there certainly were times when religious claims were consciously constructed in an attempt to persuade people to do what their political or economic leaders wanted done. Jeremiah and Amos, among others, make this same point.

Perhaps our Bibles need to have a statement similar to what one hears before controversial TV programs: "Statements expressed herein reflect the views of their authors and not necessarily those of the management."

The classic example of this is the Canaanite conquest told about in Joshua. In this war the Israelites had been told by "God" to kill all the inhabitants of certain captured towns. Surely we can admit that it is often cheaper to kill people and take what you want than it is to buy things from them. There is also a certain security you can get when you kill everyone in your way and make sure there will be no one left who is interested in seeking vengeance. There were benefits to wiping out native populations, and it is at least possible that the Israelite leaders chose to claim God's will as part of their own strategy of conquest. In any case, even if someone believes that God did tell the ancient Israelites to conduct war in this manner, it is surely too much to believe that later nations have the God-given right to kill whoever stands in the way of their territorial expansion.

In the same manner, the incident of David and Bathsheba was recorded in 2 Samuel 11:1–12:25 not to encourage us to act like David, say, by walking around on the roof so that we can watch women taking their baths. The writer intended for us to react against David's example when reading the account. In reading historical narratives, if we consider what the author was trying to show us, we can see that everything reported is not necessarily endorsed.

I realize that this interpretation of biblical history can be argued about, but the distinction I now want to make between history and legend could also be the ground for disagreements. Although more complex definitions are possible, legend is exaggerated history. In other words, legends are based on something that actually occurred, but the descriptions of either the characters or the events (or both) have been exaggerated.

History, legends, and parables are all subcategories of narratives. But distinguishing history from a parable is far easier than distinguishing history from legend. Parables have internal, literary clues to their character. For example, the phrase "There was a man" is the standard clue. Detecting legends is more a matter of judgment. I am certain that Christians will often vary on which narratives should be seen as history and which narratives were meant as legend.

In my judgment, for example, the short narrative of 2 Kings 2:23-25, in which the prophet Elisha's curse upon some boys who were making fun of his bald head, leads to two bears coming out of the woods and killing forty-two children, seems exaggerated. So too does the story about Samson catching three hundred foxes, setting their tails on fire, and letting them loose in the wheatfields of Israel's enemies (Judg 15:1-8). Legends can be found in other parts of the Bible, but to demonstrate that legends are a biblical genre, I have highlighted only two of the best examples.

Interpreting biblical history is a complex enterprise. But once a reader is willing to admit human authorship (and the implications of that authorship), one can move beyond fussing over details and go on to discovering God's presence in the Scriptures.

CHAPTER 16

Myths

There is a lot of argument about whether myths occur in the Bible. But like so many other arguments among religious people, the answer depends on how one defines the term. Nevertheless, this disagreement continues to be a very real problem since there are many definitions of the word "myth." Spending an hour in the library looking up definitions of myths will give you at least the following possibilities: (1) A myth is a story that seeks to explain why things are the way they are; (2) A myth is a story that deals with gods or goddesses; (3) A myth is a story that holds a community of people together.

Interpreting myths can be complicated, especially when one is first getting used to the concept of myth. Scholars who study literature disagree about how the term should be used. Even the experts in comparative mythology have differences of opinion about how to understand myths. In addition to that, however, is the fact that the word "myth" has such negative connotations. The word automatically upsets some readers. The primary negative connotation comes in the popular usage of the word, where a myth means a story or a belief that "just ain't so." But if we set aside this popular misconception about a myth being a false narrative, we should discover that the concept of myth allows us to make sense out of many problem passages in the Bible.

Before describing what I mean by myth, I want to stress that the common element in the three definitions given above is the word "story." Myths are a kind of narrative, having both fictional and nonfictional aspects.

It happens that the most famous Greco-Roman myths fit almost all the definitions. "Pandora's Box" is one such classical myth. After she had been created by the supreme god Zeus, Pandora was given many presents by the gods and goddesses, including a beautiful box she was told never to open. But curiosity got the better of Pandora and she opened the box. Out came a swarm of vicious reptiles, each one being named after the various troubles and disasters that afflict humanity: War, Hatred, Greed, and so on. Pandora saw these creatures escaping from the box and tried to close it. When she finally got the top to stay on, the box was empty except for the final monster, who was named "Knowledge of the Future." If that creature had escaped, no hope would have been possible. For (according to the myth) if we human beings knew the problems we would face in the future, life would be impossible. We would all give up.

"Pandora's Box" is a good example of a myth. It fits the three standard definitions. The story has gods and goddesses, it explains why so much is wrong with the world, and it is a story that the ancient Greeks shared as part of their cultural heritage. But this does not mean that the myth was looked upon as being true (if by "true" we mean "the truth, the whole truth, and nothing but the truth"). Most Greeks never thought that there had been a real Pandora. Furthermore, there are other Greek myths that also explain the source of evil. Most educated Greeks would probably have said that the myth of Pandora's box was a story that tried to illustrate how suffering is caused by humans who meddle in affairs that they are supposed to leave alone.

Truth is a difficult concept to apply to myths. It is especially difficult if our view is that "truth" must be a set of facts, accurately stated according to chronological sequence, with no facts left out. According to this very high standard of proof, "truth" can probably only be found in scientific reports about specific experiments. But we make a major mistake if we think that only scientific writing is able to express what is really true.

For example, consider the Greco-Roman fable about the fox and the sour grapes. When the fox was unable to grab the grapes he wanted, he walked away muttering that the grapes were sour. On the one hand, foxes (at least as far as we know) do not talk to themselves, and so, on one level, this fable is false. The facts are all wrong.

On the other hand, the reality of "sour grapes" is something most of us are familiar with. In fact, our trying to express the notion of "sour grapes" in straightforward prose is an excellent way to see how well the fable works at expressing a very complex human characteristic. The fable turns out to be an effective way to show the reality of this very human emotion.

In the same manner, to criticize J. R. R. Tolkien's *The Lord of the Rings* because it is based upon the fiction that there are hobbits misses the whole point of reading this story. Even though the story is not factual, it is still able to express a number of truths, important truths about friendship, loyalty, trust, and continuing with a hopeless task because it is the right thing to do.

The truth that can be expressed by a myth is similar to the truth that can be expressed by a fable, a novel, or a parable. I do not want to rule out the possibility that a myth might have some basis in fact or might be the best possible description of a historical event. (In this I think I agree with C. S. Lewis, who once remarked that the story of Jesus Christ is a myth but a true myth because the resurrection of Jesus actually occurred.) A myth can be related to history. But that relationship is incidental to the main purpose of myth, which is to tell a story in simple language in order to convey something much more profound. No matter how the myth relates to what actually happened, a good myth can tell us something both important and true.

The best clues to recognizing myths are internal ones. Is there something in a passage that is unknowable or logically impossible? By this question I do not mean to rule out miracles. Miracles recorded in the Bible usually mention witnesses and are often logically possible. Setting aside legends, most of the miracles found in historical writing do not involve logical impossibility but rather circumstantial improbability. The "mighty wind" that allowed the Israelites to escape Egypt in the Exodus is an example of such an improbable event. The event itself is not impossible but rather only very improbable. And surely the timing of such a mighty wind is what constitutes the miracle.

Finding an internal clue, especially in a narrative where the message seems more important than any historical account of the events, provides good evidence that one is reading a myth. But recognizing myths in the Bible will be influenced by our knowledge of the world. For one thing, what was once considered "history" might come to be better seen as myth. The story of Noah's ark provides an example of this reevaluation. For many hundreds of years this story was assumed to be a historical account of a universal flood and God's method for saving the animals. But a scientific approach to the study of the natural world has convinced many Christians that the biblical author was writing myth. Internal clues to the mythic nature of the story are the observations that there is no evidence for a universal flood, there was not enough room on board the ark for all the animals, there was not enough food on board, there is no mention about how the freshwater fish (or the saltwater fish) could survive in the flood waters, there is no mention of how the plants survived, and so on.

In addition to the fact that some biblical myths were once seen as history, recognizing myths may require some courage because of the added psychological pressure many religious people feel when they are challenged about their beliefs. I can remember presenting this interpretation of Noah's ark to an adult Bible study class and hearing a visiting minister make the observation that "God must have made the animals get smaller" as they went up the gangplank and then "must have put them into suspended animation" once they were led to their rooms.

I do not doubt that God could do that sort of thing. But I question the reasoning of anyone who comes up with that sort of interpretation of Noah's ark. To put it simply, that is not how the author of Genesis chose to tell the story. It seems to me that dealing with biblical passages *as they are recorded* is a much better way to read the Bible. The policy of "multiplying miracles" in order to make everything in the Bible into straightforward history (that is, inventing miracles to fill in all the historical and scientific gaps in narratives) seems like refusing to listen to the Holy Spirit. If the Holy Spirit inspired someone to write a myth, we should be willing to read the material as it was inspired.

The flip side of refusing to see any myths in the Bible is seeing too many. (I would need to be convinced that more than a few myths can be found outside the Book of Genesis.) We need to be careful before we deny the historicity of an event. Very often it does not matter whether a passage is history or myth. The message of the selection could be the same in either case. But there are times when the historicity of a passage is crucial. The accounts of Christ's resurrection I consider to be historical. Paul's analysis of the resurrection in 1 Corinthians 15 has persuaded me that if Jesus did not, in fact, rise from the dead then we have made a terrible mistake in bothering to try to lead Christian lives. I do not see that anything crucial hinges on the historicity of Noah's ark, but Christ's resurrection is a different matter.

After concluding that a particular narrative is a myth, we must go on to the task of interpreting the myth. This is not as easy as interpreting a parable. Myths can be a richer genre in that they often evoke a wide variety of feelings and ideas. But because they can have so many layers of meaning, it is easy to give them perverse interpretations.

Even though the myth of Pandora's box tells of how her curiosity led to the present unhappy state of the world, I think it is going too far to say that the mythmaker, and those who remembered the myth, hated women and blamed feminine curiosity for making a mess of the cosmos. It is true that Greco-Roman culture was male oriented and undervalued women, but that was not the primary message the mythmaker was trying to communicate. One cannot prove Greco-Roman gender bias on the basis of this myth alone. (One could demonstrate that bias fairly easily by looking at other literary and historical examples, but that is another issue.)

In the same manner, it is possible to give perverse interpretations to biblical myths as well. Consider the myth of the Fall in Genesis 3:1-24. Adam and Eve had been told not to eat of the fruit of a certain tree in the Garden of Eden. Eve was tempted by the serpent, deceived by it, ate some of the fruit, and Adam joined her for a bite. Perverse interpretations of this myth would be that this particular God wanted people to be stupid (that is, not to acquire knowledge), or that the Bible teaches that God—being jealous—has an inferiority complex, or that women are the cause of everything that is wrong with the world, and so on.

I consider these examples perverse interpretations because they are not based upon an effort to discover what the author was trying to communicate. It may be that the author was antiintellectual, narrow in his understanding of God, and a misogynist, but I do not think he was trying to communicate those aspects of his personality in telling us the myth. I think he was trying to say something about finding one's place in the universe and about recognizing that the world could have been a paradise if human beings had not tried to make themselves gods.

In general, modern readers of the Bible probably should make an initial effort to give biblical myths the benefit of a doubt. What positive message (if any) was a particular author trying to communicate? It is easy to get sidetracked by looking at how certain myths have been used to oppress intellectuals, "heretics," women, and all sorts of other people. No one who has studied the history of Christianity can deny that people calling themselves Christians have used the Bible as a club to bash those who stood in their way. But focusing only on the history of such later behavior can make us miss what the biblical authors said. It is possible that the biblical materials, including the myths, contain a great deal worth listening to.

Conclusions

Now that we have reached the end of this book exploring biblical genres, I do not want to leave a false implication that there are no other types of literature that can be found in the Bible. Scholars love to develop more and more specific subcategories within genres, and one can find other lists of biblical genres. In addition, it is likely that scholars of ancient literature may discover material or will acquire more detailed knowledge from the biblical world and give us more information about some particular genre that was commonly used in the past but died out later. For example, epic poetry was extremely popular in the ancient world, but few people write it (or read it) today.

Yet, even though further study can usually help us understand more of the Scriptures, it often happens that the scholarly study of the Bible loses all contact with the interests and concerns of Christian readers. The genres examined here were selected because I considered them the most important categories. Many of them are controversial, and some of the examples used could be argued over. But by knowing these genres, a reader has the background to start making sense of even the most difficult passages in the Bible.

After reading a biblical selection, one must ask about the kind of literature being read. Is the passage a parable, a hymn, a quotation, a myth, or something else? It is only by knowing the genre of the text that the reader can discover what the author was trying to say.

Of course, the reader still needs to use common sense. There are passages which have overlapping genres. Parables are found within narratives, commandments are found in sermons, and ethical advice is found in letters. In cases like these, the reader needs to make a decision about which genre is most important for interpreting the passage.

For example, consider the statement in Matthew 5:43, "You shall love your neighbor and hate your enemy." The genres overlap here. Jesus' statement is (1) a quotation (2) in ethical instruction (3) in a sermon (4) in a narrative. To understand Jesus here, we must realize that he was quoting that statement in order to disagree with it. When we consider the paragraph of ethical instruction that surrounds the quotation, especially the sentence that follows (Matt 5:44), "But I say to you, love your enemies, and pray for those who persecute you," we can see Jesus' overall point. Knowing that the quotation is in a sermon and in a narrative does not help us as much as knowing that it is within a section of ethical instruction.

Another example can be found in Paul's Letter to the Galatians 6:1: "Even if a person is caught in some transgression, you who are spiritual should correct that one in a gentle spirit, looking to yourself, so that you may not be tempted." This is ethical instruction (and, more specifically, advice) contained in a letter. If a reader refused to accept Paul's advice because Paul's letter was written to the Galatians over nineteen hundred years ago, that person would be missing the point. The genre of Galatians is indeed a letter. And the people who first received it made their own decisions long ago about whether they would accept Paul's advice or not. But ancient letters to dead people may still have something to say to us. In fact, if we judge Paul's advice in terms of the biblical commandments about loving one another, it seems to me that we need to follow Paul's advice even today. When it is necessary, we ought to correct one another in a gentle manner, lest we be tempted to become self-righteous. In our effort to understand Galatians 6:1, we need to recognize that the less significant genre is that of the letter and the more significant genre is that of ethical instruction.

Finding the genre that matters most is the way to make sense of passages with overlapping genres. It may turn out that we will decide that a passage in question is a myth or an exaggeration within a sermon. But does not mean that we should ignore that passage. No genre has the truth locked up. A good writer can probably communicate in several genres, and surely a divinely inspired message could be communicated within a variety of literary forms.

I am convinced that an inspired writer could have told us something important in any genre he chose to use. Furthermore, it seems to me that if God inspired someone to write a proverb or a myth, then we who read the Bible must do our best to understand those proverbs or myths. How God chose to inspire biblical writers was a decision made without my input, but I am willing to trust God's judgment. It seems to me to be the height of pride to think that we are smarter than God and able to decide beforehand that God can only communicate with us in one way. We need to let God speak through the literature we have.

I do not have an explanation for all the things that are in the Bible. There are passages I like and passages I do not like to hear. I like to be reminded that God loves me and cares about me, and I especially like to hear passages which promise me health, wealth, and public respect. But there are other parts I am less crazy about. I do not like to read about what I might need to do in order to help those around me, especially if such activity might require money, time, or effort. I am also troubled, at times, by the passages I do not understand. Could I be missing something I need to hear? And might the cause of this lack of understanding be in my intellect or in my narrow-mindedness?

This book was not meant to explain everything you always wanted to know about the Bible. It was meant to demonstrate how the knowledge of literary genres is a necessary component in any serious study of the Bible. We should always begin our study of the Scriptures by asking what the author was trying to say. Only after that can we go on to compare the author's message with our own particular circumstances. We start by seeking sense in the Bible. We end up by finding God's presence.